Knowledge Management

CARL FRAPPAOLO

Published in 2006 by   Capstone Publishing Ltd. (A Wiley company), The Atrium,
Southern Gate Chichester, West Sussex, PO19 8SQ, England

Phone   (+44) 1243 779777

Copyright © 2006   Capstone Publishing Ltd

Email (for orders and customer service enquiries): cs-books@wiley.co.uk
Visit our Home Page on www.wiley.co.uk or www.wiley.com

Reprinted March 2006

Other Wiley Editorial Offices

John Wiley & Sons Inc., 111 River Street, Hoboken, NJ 07030, USA

Jossey-Bass, 989 Market Street, San Francisco, CA 94103-1741, USA

Wiley-VCH Verlag GmbH, Boschstr. 12, D-69469 Weinheim, Germany

John Wiley & Sons Australia Ltd, 42 McDougall Street, Milton, Queensland 4064, Australia

John Wiley & Sons (Asia) Pte Ltd, 2 Clementi Loop #02-01, Jin Xing Distripark, Singapore 129809

John Wiley & Sons Canada Ltd, 22 Worcester Road, Etobicoke, Ontario, Canada M9W 1L1

Wiley also publishes its books in a variety of electronic formats. Some content that appears in print may not be available in electronic books.

CIP Catalogue records for this book are available from the British Library and the US Library of Congress

ISBN10: 1-84112-705-1 (PB)   ISBN13: 978-1-84112-705-7 (PB)

Typeset in 9/11pt Garamond by Laserwords Private Limited, Chennai, India
Printed and bound in Great Britain by TJ International, Padstow, Cornwall
This book is printed on acid-free paper responsibly manufactured from sustainable forestry in which at least two trees are planted for each one used for paper production.

To: GEF for his silent and constant support of my efforts.

Contents

Introduction to Knowledge Management

Knowledge management was the business and technology term *du jour* of 1997. What is its current state? This introduction takes a current perspective on knowledge management. It includes:

» identification of currently popular knowledge-based applications;
» current debate over the value and reality of knowledge management; and
» listing of organizations whose intellectual capital represents significant value to their bottom line.

"If HP Knew what HP Knows we would be three times more profitable."

Lew Platt, former CEO of Hewlett Packard

1997: knowledge management (KM) suddenly emerged from the world of academia and became a burning issue for business and technology leaders. Two short years later, technology media lost interest. And the business press moved on to B2B mania.

In fact, some industry pundits have announced that knowledge management is dead. This of course brings to my mind the Mark Twain quote, "Rumors of my death are greatly exaggerated." Knowledge management did not die; it has been quietly smoldering within corporations. In practice, knowledge management is rising like the phoenix, with great velocity. It has morphed into a series of killer applications including portals, e-learning, e-analysis, and content management. Corporations such as Northrop Grumman, Hallmark, Pillsbury, Pfizer, and Buckman Labs have successful KM practices – and these are the companies that are willing to talk about their efforts. Add to this group the scores of enterprises that have implemented KM under the umbrella of a portal or an e-learning initiative and the number is easily quadrupled.

But the nay-sayers and doubting Thomases persist. While knowledge management has slowly matured within global organizations, familiarity has also bred skepticism. The hype fueled by vendors anxious to position their respective technologies as a knowledge panacea has been challenged by pertinent questions posed in mainstream media. Trade publications such as *MIS* and *CIO* magazines have launched attacks on the fundamental concepts behind knowledge management. The May 2001 issue of *CIO* featured an article that positioned KM as a "solid concept that fell in with the wrong company." "Unfortunately, this is knowledge management today – a good idea gone awry," said *CIO*. "KM has fallen victim to a mixture of bad implementation practices and software vendors eager to turn a complex process into a pure technology play. The result: like many a business concept, KM has evolved from a hot buzzword to a phrase that now evokes more skepticism than enthusiasm."

This position on KM is not the only viewpoint in the media. On the other side of the debate, specialist KM press such as *Knowledge*

Management Magazine paint a more positive picture. In a study commissioned by *Knowledge Management Magazine* for its May 2001 issue, companies were said to "put a high priority on the success of [KM] deployments: executive managers lead more than 40 per cent of all KM deployments." Other conclusions from the study supported the positive spin, but with a voice of reality. The survey found that a pivotal issue in migrating to a knowledge strategy is the creation of a culture to support trust and collaboration.

The debate could rage on forever. Indeed, in the academic world, which is the root of KM, the debate over whether knowledge can be properly managed will forever rage on. This title will not participate in this exercise. The point is that knowledge management has demonstrated an impact on business. We must move beyond the academic and focus on practical, albeit imperfect applications of knowledge management strategies and practices in business. In a 2002 online discussion on KM chaired by myself and hosted by AOK, Debra Amidon, chairman and CEO of ENTOVATION International Ltd (a global innovation research and consulting network), put it best: "So many of the well-intended knowledge programs are dwelling on the unnecessary questions, spending inordinate precious intellectual talent on sub-optimal activities and not realizing that what we are creating is a dynamic management system for a viable business strategy, not just a storage capacity for accumulated knowledge ... albeit sometimes useful." She stresses that KM can be about academic debate and discussion, or about taking calculated strategic action to harness and leverage as much intellectual capital as possible to advance business and scientific causes.

I have witnessed knowledge management practices make bottom line differences to organizations ranging from government to manufacturing. Call it KM, call it an executive information portal, call it content management, call it intellectual capital – it is still knowledge management and it makes a difference.

KM enables taking informed action in previously unencountered/unknown circumstances. In the current economic climate, although companies are careful about undertaking new technology initiatives, they are realizing that leveraging the *already* accumulated corporate intellectual property is by far the lowest-cost way available to increase their competitive stature. In a knowledge-based economy, knowledge management is the critical element of a business strategy that will allow the organization to accelerate the rate at which it handles new market challenges and opportunities, and it does so by leveraging its most precious of resources, collective know-how, talent and experience – intellectual capital.

Some forward-thinking companies list intellectual capital as a line item in their annual reports. One need only look at the deltas between the market capitalization of organizations such as GE, and Google and their net worth to appreciate the value that is placed on knowledge management (in each case intellectual capital can be attributed to 82 percent, and 98 percent of these companies' capitalization respectively). Rules and tenets that were once central to the formation of organizations, employment, and work itself are being challenged. Still not convinced? Consider that in 1995, IBM bought Lotus for $3.5 billion. This was 14 times Lotus's book value. What was IBM paying for? In a word, knowledge: knowledge of the collaboration market, of the knowledge management market, and an ability to *act* on that knowledge. Organizations are no longer valued solely for what they have done – but the potential of what they might be able to do. A new breed of organizational manager is emerging, valued for their ability to leverage knowledge to make unparalleled advances in their organization's ability to innovate, compete and connect with their customers. The promise and interest in knowledge management is not in knowing – but in being able to act creatively based on what you know. Therein lies the flaw in Lew Platt's quote that started this introduction. Companies are valued and succeed not just for what they know, but their ability to leverage what they know creatively and proactively (see the definition of knowledge management in Chapter 2 for more detail on the role of proactive innovation in KM). This is the asset that pushes market capitalization beyond net worth. Microsoft is not valued so much for its current products and market share, but for its potential to leverage the vast intellectual resources – read experience and know-how – it has amassed. Bill Gates was quoted to say that the web browser was not going to become popular. He was sure that users would insist on serious desktop machines. But, when the market began to prove him wrong, Gates reassessed Microsoft's capacity to innovate and met the then market leader Netscape head-on with Explorer. The rest is an evolving history. Similarly, when it witnessed the rise of the Internet, it was Sun Microsystems' ability to quickly reposition a stalling, virtually unknown platform-independent interface and programming language product as the Internet programming language Java that exemplifies the value of Sun – not the Java product itself. This type of innovation is the fruit of knowledge management, and the reason it is a critical element to business success in the current business climate.

But if innovation is the fruit, we must not forget the infrastructure behind knowledge management. In this regard, Lew Platt was right. You still need to know what you know. The raw goods of intellectual capital – experience and know-how – must be channeled and made available, otherwise innovation can be hampered. This is a very real problem for many organizations. Consider the issue that NASA faces. Virtually everyone involved with the Apollo project is now either retired or dead. With them went the know-how on how to land a man on the moon. While the planned approaches were captured, the dynamically acquired knowledge base that emerged through facing the challenges that each Apollo mission presented were not captured anywhere but in the brains of these now departed employees. PriceWaterhouse Coopers reported that 50 percent of their employees are typically in their first or last year with the firm. In our volatile job market, where and how is the intellectual capital being captured?

Knowledge management represents a means by which to capture and monitor ever-developing bodies of intellectual capital, and to promote its leverage by communities of practice. KM promotes practices and technologies that facilitate the efficient creation and exchange of knowledge on an organization-wide level. When you extend this definition to include partners, suppliers and customers as well, you extend the KM practice into the collaborative commerce space. The advent of the Internet as a worldwide common interface is making this vision possible, but it also raises the bar on the scope of success and failure. Given the potential plethora of knowledge available both inside and outside the organization, any business strategy today that ignores the tenets of knowledge management is a formula for certain failure. As Dr Peter Drucker put it in his *Managing in a Time of Great Change*, "Knowledge has become the key economic resource and the dominate – and perhaps the only – source of competitive advantage."

02

What is Knowledge Management?

Knowledge management brings to mind many things to many people. But in a business setting, a practical definition prevails. The basic definition of knowledge management is discussed, as well as those concepts critical to its effective deployment. This section examines:

» the effect of knowledge management;
» how knowledge management is different from information management;
» types of knowledge;
» the knowledge chain and its role in measuring the success of knowledge practices; and
» the basic knowledge management applications.

"A little knowledge that acts is worth more than much knowledge that is idle."

Kahlil Gibran, The Prophet

Defining knowledge management is not a simple issue. It is not a technology, although technology should be exploited as an enabler. It is not a directive, although strategic leadership is imperative to successful knowledge management. It is not a business strategy, although one aligned with the tenets of knowledge management must exist. It requires a culture that promotes faith in collectively sharing and thinking. But, culture alone will not render a vital knowledge management practice. It is perhaps the lack of a singular definition that has delayed the more wide-scale deployment of knowledge management.

Put succinctly:

Knowledge management is the leveraging of collective wisdom to increase responsiveness and innovation.

It is important that you discern from this definition three critical points. This definition implies that three criteria must be met before information can be considered knowledge.

» Knowledge is connected. It exists in a collection (collective wisdom) of multiple experiences and perspectives.
» Knowledge management is a catalyst. It is an action – leveraging. Knowledge is always relevant to environmental conditions, and stimulates action in response to these conditions. Information that does not precipitate action of some kind is not knowledge. In the words of Peter Drucker, "Knowledge for the most part exists only in application."
» Knowledge is applicable in unencountered environments. Information becomes knowledge when it is used to address novel situations for which no direct precedent exists. Information that is merely "plugged in" to a previously encountered model is not knowledge and lacks innovation.

It is important, therefore, to draw a clear line of distinction between information management and knowledge management. Both are important to an organization's success, but each addresses different needs and requires different approaches. Information management consists of predetermined responses to anticipated stimuli. Knowledge management consists of innovative responses to new opportunities and challenges. In business, planned responses to controlled stimuli can be, and have been, automated through traditional IT approaches. Knowledge-based solutions, however, focus on the application of innovative new responses in a volatile work environment, as illustrated in Fig. 2.1. Knowledge must be internalized; it co-exists with intelligence and experience and emanates at the points where decisions are made. For this reason, the primary repository for knowledge is people's heads (at least until we agree that machines have intelligence). Electronic and paper-based "knowledge repositories," then, are merely intermediate storage points for information en route between people's heads.

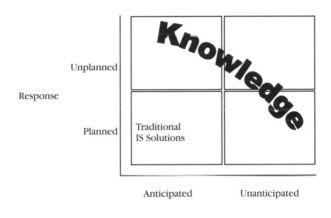

Fig. 2.1 The focus of knowledge-based solutions in a dynamic work environment.

But there is more needed to develop a complete understanding of knowledge and knowledge management than these basic premises. Understanding knowledge management begins with two basic characteristics: knowledge complexity and knowledge applications. The former refers to the physical manifestations and depth of knowledge available, the latter to approaches to connecting knowledge to people and processes. Each is discussed below.

THE COMPLEXITY OF KNOWLEDGE: FROM EXPLICIT TO TACIT

All knowledge can be classified according to its complexity on a continuum from explicit to tacit. Michael Polanyi identified the distinction between these two types of knowledge in 1966 (Polanyi, M., *The Tacit Dimension*, Routledge & Kegan Paul, 1966).

Explicit knowledge is knowledge that is articulated in formal language and easily transmitted among individuals both synchronously and asynchronously. Tacit knowledge, on the other hand, is personal knowledge embedded in individual experience and involving such intangible factors as personal belief, perspective, instinct, and values.

Explicit knowledge is referred to as information in the context of our discussion. The challenge of explicit knowledge is one of handling the sheer volume of information that is available. On the other hand, while tacit knowledge potentially can represent great value to the organization, it is, by its very nature, far more difficult to capture and diffuse. The challenges represented by each type of knowledge at a very high level are the same – to build a bridge between seekers and providers of knowledge. But from a practical level the challenges are very different. Explicit knowledge can be adequately transferred with the help of electronic tools. On the other hand, the most efficient way to convey tacit knowledge throughout the organization is face to face. Practices such as apprenticeships, mentoring and communities of practice prove effective.

For decades, organizations have focused their information technology investments on explicit knowledge, rather than tacit knowledge (see Chapter 4 for more details on technology approaches to handling Explicit knowledge). There are three reasons for this: first, explicit knowledge is often conveyed as a standard part of most transaction-based information systems; second, explicit knowledge is much easier to convey and capture than tacit knowledge; and, third, we have an inherent mistrust of anything that cannot be conveyed objectively and quantified (i.e. tacit knowledge). The primary challenge when facing explicit knowledge is to manage its volume, ensure its relevance and quality, and make it easily accessible – in a phrase, handling infoglut.

There is no doubt that tacit knowledge plays a pivotal role in distinguishing companies and poising them for success. For this reason, an ability to expand the level of tacit knowledge throughout an organization through its proactive sharing is regarded as one of the core objectives of knowledge management. It also happens to be one of the most challenging. For tacit knowledge, the challenge is to formulate the knowledge into communicable form. But, tacit knowledge defies being systematically cataloged and made available in an asynchronous manner; by its very definition, it is forever changing, growing and being reshaped by the owners' latest experiences. Tacit knowledge should be approached with greater scrutiny and a determination made as to what degree or depth the knowledge can be captured or tracked.

From tacit to implicit

In some cases, knowledge believed to be tacit is only so labeled because no one has ever taken the time or energy to codify the knowledge. Users may be too quick to reply, "It's just too difficult to explain; it defies explanation." This is a real problem and one not easily resolved. You must determine if bodies of uncoded knowledge can be captured and made explicit. However, it is critical to first be sure that a culture that promotes and supports knowledge sharing is in place, or users may recoil by hoarding even more of what they know (see more on establishing and measuring culture via a knowledge audit in Chapter 10). In any case, it is imperative that you appreciate that perfect management of tacit knowledge is not possible. Do not get preoccupied with getting it perfect, because you could miss out on great success without ever achieving 100 percent accuracy.

Certain knowledge can be harvested from its owner and codified in such a way as to make it more readily sharable. Using such a process you can create a third type of knowledge in the organization: implicit knowledge. The value and leveragability of implicit knowledge is vast. However, an organization must take several strategic steps in order to position it adequately. First, the sources and nature of the implicit bodies of knowledge must be identified and quantified (this is where a knowledge audit proves useful – see Chapter 10). Getting to implicit knowledge mandates taking a second look at all so-called tacit knowledge resources to determine whether that knowledge could be codified if it were subjected to some type of mining and translation process. Then, it requires implementing that mining/translation process. Often, much of the work done in businesses is not in the deep tacit realm. Rather, it is a logical, methodical thinking process that simply is not recognized as such, even by the thinker.

Implicit knowledge management employs tools, techniques and methodologies that capture these previously elusive processes and make them more generally available to the organization. Thus, the thought processes used by your best thinkers become a leveragable asset for the organization. Again, I must stress that not all tacit knowledge can be transfigured into implicit knowledge. There will always be bodies of know-how and experience that remain tacit.

Also tacit knowledge is not an effective way to achieve alignment between personal and organizational values (storytelling and mentoring are better ways to achieve value alignment). Finally, there are some intellectual assets too novel for capture and transfer. The goal of implicit knowledge management is to determine how much of the tacit knowledge in your organization defies any form of codification, and to mine that which does not.

GRAPEVINES, COMMUNITIES OF PRACTICES AND THE INFORMAL KNOWLEDGE NETWORK

Where knowledge legitimately exists in tacit bodies, knowledge-based strategies should not focus on collecting and disseminating information, but rather on creating a mechanism for practitioners to easily identify and reach out to other practitioners. Such mechanisms, like communities of practice, have special characteristics. They emerge of their own accord: they collaborate directly, use one another as sounding boards, and teach one another. They are built on a bond of obvious *trust* – a key word for any knowledge management solution.

Communities of this sort are difficult to construct and easy to destroy but, in my experience, almost always exist in every organization, both formally and informally. Where present, it behooves you to recognize them and encourage them, support them. They are among the most important structures of any organization where thinking matters, but they almost inevitably undermine its formal structures and strictures if improperly managed. Remember that knowledge is connected. For information to be transformed into knowledge you must recognize, support and administer the connections and, most importantly, the people, who are the ultimate owners of all knowledge. (In Chapter 4 the technology approach to personal profiling is explained, an approach to tracking and defining what individuals seem to exhibit interest in, or knowledge about. These profiles are used to intermediate knowledge seekers with knowledge providers, establishing online communities.)

As stated in Chapter 1, organizational strength does not come from knowledge of the past per se; rather, it comes from the ability to regenerate knowledge of the organization, its processes and its markets – to take timely innovative action on an ongoing basis. This is where knowledge management clearly differentiates itself from other approaches to governing expertise such as reengineering (for more detail on the differences between knowledge management and reengineering and TQM, see Chapter 3). Knowledge management assumes a constant vigilance of change, and encourages constant modification – innovation – at a rate that at least keeps pace with changing market dynamics.

Make no mistake, knowledge management emphasizes the re-use of previous experiences and practices, but its focus is on mapping these to the changing landscape of the market. If that sounds simple, then try answering the following question: What is your organization's core competency? If you answered with a product name, you are shackled by the past. The chances are, if you answered in this manner, you are referring to a most successful product. Success forms the most restrictive shackles. Your competency must outlive product success. Products should exist at the vortex of the whirlpool – constantly changing. Your core competencies should live at the outer limits of the whirlpool.

Knowledge management suggests that an organization makes a subtle yet profound shift – from relying on its ''experience'' (or knowledge of the past) to relying on its ''competencies'' (or resourcefulness to handle the future). Knowledge of the past is only valuable inasmuch as it provides a perspective on the future. Competency, on the other hand, equips the organization to respond to as yet unknown forces for change.

THE KNOWLEDGE CHAIN

Fundamental to the practical definition of knowledge management is the concept of the knowledge chain. The knowledge chain was first recognized by Koulopoulos, Toms and Spinello in doing research for their book *Corporate Instinct*. There are four links in the knowledge chain that determine the uniqueness and longevity of any organization. These four links are:

» internal awareness;
» internal responsiveness;
» external responsiveness; and
» external awareness.

The knowledge chain (K-chain) is a series of interactions that constitute an organization's cycle of innovation. Knowledge management creates permeability between the four cells of the K-chain and accelerates the speed of innovation. The four stages of the knowledge chain define the flow of knowledge through an enterprise, as shown in Fig. 2.2. The ability to quickly traverse through the four cells of the knowledge chain is the essence of the benefit of knowledge management.

Internal awareness

In its simplest terms, internal awareness is the ability of an organization to quickly assess its inventory of skills and core competency. It is the awareness of past history in terms of talent, know-how, interaction, process performance, and communities of practice. Strong emphasis on functional organization structures, which often permeate traditional companies, inhibits the development of internal awareness. Organizations with a rigid functional structure most often define their core competency as their products and services, not their skills. Strong internal awareness is built on an ongoing challenge of what is done and a focus on what is possible. This is what Peter Drucker refers to as "organizational abandonment."

Internal responsiveness

Internal responsiveness is the ability to exploit internal awareness. An organization may be well aware of its strengths and market demand,

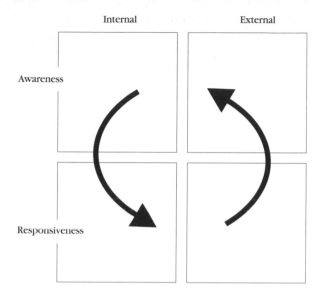

Fig. 2.2 Movement through the four cells of the knowledge chain.

but if it is not able to adequately effect change within itself quickly enough to meet market requirements, its competencies are virtually moot. In a study conducted by Delphi Group of 350 respondents, 30 percent indicated that they had greater external awareness than internal responsiveness. In other words, these organizations felt that "we are better at understanding the market then we are at rallying and coordinating our own resources in response." No wonder 50 percent of respondents to the same survey indicated that a good idea had more chance of resulting in a new startup or ending up at a competitor before their own organization acted on it.

Internal responsiveness considers how quickly competencies can be translated into actions to bring a product to market or respond to a customer need. There's no point in responding quickly, though, if it's too late. Reengineering, for example, is often little more than overcompensation for a company's inability to respond to a series of small market shifts over an extended period of time (see Chapter 3 for more detail on the differences between reengineering and knowledge management). It must be stressed that successful KM is the coordinated ability to exercise internal responsiveness based on what is known via continuous awareness (both external and internal) and perception through all levels and functional areas.

External responsiveness

Simply put, external responsiveness is the ability to best meet the requirements of the market. When all is said and done, an organization's ability to better satisfy this cell in the knowledge chain than its competitors will determine its success or failure. External responsiveness is measured by the ability to effectively respond to opportunities and threats outside of the organization in a timely manner. This is the essence of competitive advantage – a level of responsiveness to environmental conditions that is significantly faster than that of its competitors.

External awareness

External awareness is the mirror image of internal awareness. It is the organization's ability to understand how the market perceives the value associated with its products and services, to understand who are its customers, what those customers want, who are their competitors, competencies of competitors, market trends, competitive actions, government regulations, and any other relevant market forces that exist outside the organization itself. When coupled with internal awareness, external awareness may lead to entirely new markets.

External awareness is one of the cornerstones of the Internet, where new business models are sprouting up at an unprecedented pace. The velocity of the Internet provides an incredible opportunity to act upon the market's reaction to new products. However, new models for capturing market responses are just as critical. For example, Amazon.com's ability to capture buying trends of many book buyers and then use these to suggest books with similar themes and authors is the very essence of external awareness coupled with external responsiveness. A body of knowledge (customer buying habits) is productized and offered as a value-add, differentiating the online bookstore from its brick and mortar counterpart.

External awareness is more than just a function of extensive focus groups and market research. These provide testimony to what the market needs today, or yesterday, rather than what it will need in the future. In the worst case it provides only the answers that the market thinks you want to hear. The "classic" example is that of New Coke, which, despite heavy market analysis, proved the ultimate folly of most focus groups. As markets move at an ever-faster pace, traditional market research is reaching the end of its useful life cycle.

The knowledge chain of an organization is often a mix of positive and negative attributes. Table 2.1 depicts the four cells of the knowledge chain within an organization that is not knowledge driven; this is, therefore, a typical profile of a poorly positioned enterprise.

Table 2.1 Status of the knowledge chain within an organisation that is not knowledge driven.

	Internal	External
Awareness	Poor internal awareness is indicated by extensive use of organization charts, management by edict, lack of knowledge sharing, and static policies and procedures. Focus is on product lines and process awareness and intimacy with core competencies and experiences learned.	Protracted customer feedback loops result from belabored market research and a reliance on product branding. Few opportunities are given to react directly and dynamically with customers and prospects. Customers are looked at in terms of sales volume only. There is little effort to "predict" the market.
Responsiveness	New ideas are stifled by reliance on how things "should get done," a hierarchical command and control structure, and extensive departmental organization.	Slow distribution channels result in standardized products, long durations between innovation cycles, and extensive emphasis on internal rate of return.

In organizations that are knowledge driven, all four cells are permeable, allowing the immediate transfer of knowledge between the cells. Table 2.2 illustrates the four cells of the knowledge chain within an organization that leverages knowledge; this is, then, a typical profile of an exemplary, well-positioned enterprise.

Table 2.2 Status of the knowledge chain within an organisation that leverages knowledge.

	Internal	External
Awareness	Always *collectively* aware of its strengths and weaknesses across structural silos and functional boundaries. Experiences are openly communicated; focus is on competencies and talents, not products.	Constantly removing filters between the market and its innovative capacity to form partnerships with prospects and customers. Forward-thinking organizations even form partnerships with would-be competitors (see the discussion on vortals in Chapter 5).
Responsiveness	Able to instantly organize skills based on an unfiltered assessment of the internal awareness of its resources and external market demands/opportunities.	Meet the market on its own terms – even when the market cannot articulate these and a clear return is not present. Focus is on customer service, as opposed to pricing, and productizing knowledge as a value-add to the customer.

In summary, success is not gained by excelling in any one of these quadrants, but by proficiency in each and, more importantly, measured by the speed with which knowledge flows through these four links (see Chapter 6 for a discussion on return on time).

As stated before, this flow of knowledge across the links is about the connections that exist between bodies of knowledge, actions taken and knowledge known, and knowledge seekers and knowledge providers. These connections are best understood by viewing them in terms of the four basic applications of knowledge management.

KNOWLEDGE MANAGEMENT APPLICATIONS

The four key applications of knowledge management are based on a model that regards knowledge management's primary role as the sharing of knowledge throughout the organization in a way that each individual or group understands the knowledge with sufficient depth and in sufficient context as to apply it effectively in decision making and innovation.

These four applications of knowledge management are:

» intermediation;
» externalization;
» internalization; and
» cognition.

These applications are affected across all bodies of knowledge, ranging from the explicit to the tacit. Each application has a particular focus, but is in turn best realized through integration with the other applications. In Chapter 4 the technologies available to address each of the knowledge applications are overviewed. But first, it is important to understand the applications themselves and their role in a knowledge environment.

Intermediation

Intermediation is the connection between knowledge and people. Intermediation refers to the brokerage function of bringing together those who seek a certain piece of knowledge with those who are able to provide that piece of knowledge. It is a fundamental step in internal and external responsiveness. Its role is to "match" a knowledge seeker with the optimal personal source(s) of knowledge for that seeker. Two types of intermediation are common, asynchronous and synchronous.

Asynchronous intermediation occurs when externalization and internalization do not occur simultaneously. In this case, an external knowledge repository stores the knowledge while it is in transit. Knowledge is captured in the knowledge base, often before a specific need for that knowledge elsewhere in the organization has arisen. When a knowledge seeker requires that knowledge, the knowledge base can be searched and the relevant knowledge extracted. This approach is typically best suited to explicit knowledge.

Synchronous intermediation occurs when externalization and internalization occur simultaneously. Knowledge is not stored while being transferred. Knowledge provider and knowledge seeker engage in direct communication. The challenge is to match knowledge providers with knowledge seekers intuitively and in a timely manner. This approach is far more common in tacit knowledge transfer.

Externalization

Externalization is the connection of knowledge to knowledge. It refers to the process of capturing knowledge in an external repository and organizing the knowledge according to some classification framework or ontology. A map or structure of the knowledge collection is provided as a facilitator to knowledge discovery. It is focused on bringing order to internal and external awareness.

Far too many organizations focus their efforts on how to get knowledge out of their knowledge management systems and too few, if any, focus on getting knowledge into the system. A knowledge management system, like an ecosystem, cannot be constantly depleted of its resource without constant replenishment. There are two fundamental components to externalization: the capture and storage of the knowledge in a suitable repository, and the classification or organization of the knowledge.

Capture and storage can take the form of a database, a document, or a videotape. The repository for this knowledge should be appropriate for the kind of knowledge being dealt with. For example, highly numerate data may best be stored in a structured database, while visual knowledge may best be captured using videotape.

Classification or organization of the knowledge is the more difficult of the two functions. It relies on the knowledge possessed by the knowledge provider to shape the classification of the information into the most usable form. The aim here is to make the knowledge digestible to the knowledge seeker in the most efficient way possible. (For more information, see the discussion on portals in Chapter 4 and the discussion on the dilemma of organization in Chapter 10.)

Internalization

Internalization is the connection of knowledge to query. It is the extraction of knowledge from an externalized repository, and filtering it to provide personal relevance to the knowledge seeker. Closely tied to an externalized knowledge base, internalization reshapes the knowledge base specifically to address the focal point of the query issuer.

Cognition

Cognition is the linking of knowledge to process. It is the process of making or mapping decisions based on available knowledge. Cognition is the application of knowledge that has been exchanged through the preceding three functions. It is a highly proactive form of internal and external responsiveness. In its simplest form, cognition is achieved by applying experience to determine the most suitable outcome to an unprecedented event, opportunity or challenge.

KEY LEARNING POINTS

» Knowledge management is more about action than being.
» Knowledge management deals with the unanticipated stimuli and creative unplanned reactions.
» Knowledge types:
  » explicit;
  » tacit; and
  » implicit.
» The knowledge chain – a means by which to rate your organization's:
  » internal awareness;
  » external awareness;

» internal responsiveness; and

» external responsiveness.

» The basic applications of knowledge management are:

  » intermediation – brokering knowledge owner to knowledge seeker;

  » externalization – capturing and categorizing knowledge;

  » internalization – retrieving knowledge in a personal manner; and

  » cognition – applying knowledge to the business process.

03

The Evolution of Knowledge Management

Knowledge is as old as time itself. But as a formalized business practice, it finds its roots in the educated workforce that arose out of WWII. From this time, it has evolved into a series of practices and philosophical beliefs. This section traces the evolution of knowledge management over the last 50-odd years, highlighting major milestones and thinkers along the way, including:

» the advent of the knowledge worker;
» the discovery of intellectual capital as a tangible asset;
» the types of intellectual capital;
» the initial definition of knowledge types;
» the difference between knowledge management and reengineering; and
» the technological timeline.

"Now the definition of manager is someone who makes knowledge productive."

Peter Drucker

One could argue that knowledge management began with the first cave paintings, or the first use of spoken communication. But this is clearly exercise for the philosophical and academic side of knowledge management. This title focuses on the application of formal procedures and products to proactively leverage know-how within organized business practices. But even this is perhaps a bit too broad. I recall an incident on a plane journey a few years ago when the person seated next to me asked what I did for a living. After my explanation, he proceeded to tell me that, as an office supply salesperson, he too was in the knowledge management game. I will not argue now, as I did not then, that in the broadest sense, folders, pencils and paper are a form of knowledge capture and therefore can play a role in knowledge management. But, again, this title is concerned more with the specific business focus of driving innovation through proactively incentivizing knowledge sharing.

In this regard, the roots of knowledge management can be traced back to a reaction to the state of business in North America in the middle of the twentieth century, when the first wave of post-war college graduates reached the workforce. Funded by the heavy investment of the GI Bill, and the enormous collection of wartime scientific discovery, this newly minted workforce had an edge unlike any other generation – higher education. The steady incline in educated workers and the coincident increase in institutions of higher education created a steamroller that may well account for the singular most compelling need for knowledge management. Certainly it was the genesis of the modern day knowledge economy. At the time, American business culture was marked by very high levels of bureaucratization, organizational segmentation, and impersonalized – indeed depersonalized – environments. Hordes of writers and social scientists warned that the average worker, whether blue- or white-collar, felt trapped in stultifying jobs, toiling away only because there were bills to pay and mortgages to be met. Books chronicling this alienation, especially William Allan Whyte's *The Organization Man* and Sloan Wilson's *The*

Man in the Gray Flannel Suit, were bestsellers in the 1950s. They spoke for a generation of workers.

Simultaneously, the nations of Europe and Asia had recovered from their total devastation from WWII, and were becoming important players on the world market. Many of these new enterprises, inspired by the rebuilding of their businesses (literally), began to introduce new approaches to organizing and running businesses. Their employees were more involved in job definition and planning. As management and labor worked together, an obsession with quality went beyond sloganeering, perhaps in a reaction to reinstate their prowess against American business that won the war a decade or more before. Americans began to hear stories of Japanese workers gathering before the workday to exercise and sing company songs.

The market share held by American companies in many industries – steel, electronics, automobiles, shipbuilding, to name but a few – was shrinking. Moreover, there was a sense that most companies just didn't work; they were inefficient, fragmented, and resistant to new ideas. What had started as a very smart way to run a company soon became the ball and chain of American industry.

Thus the world business climate felt pressures coming from Asia, which were picked up and confronted by America, and later championed in Europe as well. It is perhaps impractical to identify when the knowledge management practice began exactly. It was under the changing business climate of the mid 1900s that several schools of thought began to emerge. Though predominately brought to the forefront through academic publications, these were typically based on real-world reviews of best and worst practices.

Each of these publications provided insight that furthered the cause and definition of knowledge management. Among the notable events and publications were the following.

In 1959, Peter Drucker coined the term "knowledge worker" in a book called *Landmarks of Tomorrow* (Harper, New York). He proposed that a new working class was rising from the industrial workers. As mentioned above, he saw this new breed of worker emerging out of a population with unprecedented levels of education. These workers, Drucker purported, had a good deal of formal education and the ability to acquire and apply theoretical and analytical knowledge.

In 1966, Michael Polanyi clarified the premise of knowledge and defined the differences between tacit and explicit knowledge. Focus began to develop not only on the value of knowledge, but on how human beings acquire and deploy knowledge. He focused attention on tacit knowledge and premised that it was the source of all forms of knowledge. His treatise was the beginning of appreciation that knowledge cannot exist without direct human interaction and therefore is more than information management (for a more detailed discussion, see Chapter 2).

In 1982, two relatively unknown management consultants, Thomas J. Peters and Robert H. Waterman Jr, published *In Search of Excellence: Lessons from America's Best-Run Companies*. This book was eye opening. It showed that organizations thriving in a brutally competitive environment shared a set of common values and practices, despite wide variations in size, mission, product, and customer base.

In 1985, Paul Strassmann published *Information Payoff*. This book offered a clear and targeted look at how investments in information technology can be justified, and provided qualitative measures to determine the impact of information technology on productivity. Strassmann also proposed the theory that no company could remain productive unless it had in place a means by which to measure and appreciate the value of human capital. The concept that knowledge as an identifiable, measurable asset began to emerge.

In 1992 Michael Hammer and James Champy published *Reengineering the Corporation*, their manifesto for a reengineering revolution. This book awoke the business world, stating that the crisis was so desperate that "obliteration" was the only adequate antidote for the ineffectual corporation. So much of this was dogma and charismatic "vision-building." CEOs and stockholders bought into the charisma, and short -term gains resulted as quality and reengineering movements raced through corporations. Hatchets came down en masse on the front office workers. While one cannot underestimate the impact that the reengineering movement had on the global corporate world, in its ability to make management realize that the old way of doing things needed to be challenged, it fell short in heralding one of the most basic and valuable features of knowledge management: continuous innovation and learning. Indeed, to appreciate the value of knowledge management, it is helpful to compare it to reengineering.

Clearly, for many organizations in the early 90s, the entrée to knowledge management was a global focus on reengineering. Reengineering demonstrated that the age-old rules that had ensured success for so long now seemed insufficient to stop a gradual slide in profitability. Established rules and procedures of operation begin to lose their effectiveness. Painfully aware that there was discontinuity between the market environment and an organization's learned response, many managers initiated radical reengineering initiatives, obliterating the established corporate procedures and rules, and rebuilt strategies and business processes to address the new business environment.

While reengineering served to rejuvenate companies around the globe, many made a fatal mistake – they replaced an outdated, invalid corporate knowledge bank with a new, soon-to-be invalid corporate knowledge bank. Reengineering assumed that a single one-time fix to a situation was the answer. Reengineering mentalities created viscous cycles, in which solutions soon became new problems. Why? Reengineering fails to take into consideration the ongoing and rapid change that characterizes today's markets.

By the mid 1990s, fueled by an increasing published body of works on the subject, management began to recognize knowledge as the key differentiating factor for organizations. Differentiators such as "quality" and "customer satisfaction" and "innovations" were slowly being recognized as tangible, critical assets of the organization. Innovation was quickly turning into the core competitive mandate.

Knowledge management proponents reacting to reengineering realized that mechanisms needed to be put in place by which their organization could break free from the mentality of complacency. Competitiveness was not something to be addressed once, waiting for its edge to be lost and then reengineered once again. Reengineering provided a short-term fix, at best. But because it assumed that the market conditions it addressed would not change, it soon created a memory of how things were – the out-dated procedures, products and processes. Unlike reengineering, knowledge management assumes a constant vigilance, encourages constant modification and innovation – at a rate that at least keeps pace with changing market dynamics.

Proponents of knowledge management assumed that change in the market was not only inevitable, but increasingly occurring.

And so it was, in the late 1990s, that the intellectual and business communities collided on a knowledge management focus and the business concept behind knowledge became mainstream. In the mid through late 1990s, several breakthrough events and treatises emerged. Leif Edvinsson became the first chief knowledge officer (CKO) in the world, working for the Swedish-based Skandia Corporation. Edvinsson emerged to become a leading authority on the subject of intellectual capital, and demonstrated how assets such as intellectual capital, innovation and customer satisfaction could be included on a corporate balance sheet. In 1997, he published, together with Michael S. Malone, the definitive book on intellectual capital, *Realizing Your Company's True Value by Finding Its Hidden Brainpower.*

In Japan, Ikujiro Nonaka had a similar focus. In 1995, with the publication of *The Knowledge Creating Company*, he introduced the world to "organizational knowledge creation," defined as the capability of a company as a whole to create new knowledge, disseminate it throughout the organization, and embody it in products, services, and systems. This process underlined the basic difference between knowledge management and reengineering – continuous and incremental innovation and growth.

Throughout this time period, Thomas Stewart, who had recently joined *Fortune* magazine, wrote countless articles. These brought a business focus and clarity to the concept of intellectual capital. In 1997 he published *Intellectual Capital: The New Wealth of Organizations*. This book shed further light on the knowledge age economy, with a direct message to the corporate world.

This is but a sampling. Throughout this time period, publications focusing on the business value of knowledge management flourished, from writers such as James Brian Quinn, Thomas Davenport, Peter Senge, Paul Romer and Dr Karl-Erik Sveiby (see Chapter 8 for more details on these authorities and their peers).

By 1995, knowledge management was a thriving topic of business discussion. Conferences and seminars proliferated. The Knowledge Management Consortium was founded. Why? And what has happened since? So far we have looked at the cerebral history of knowledge management. While I am not proposing that knowledge management is about – or owes its notoriety to – technology, the explosive interest in knowledge management in the mid to late 90s was clearly fueled by an evolving technology world.

As the technology timeline illustrates (Fig. 3.1), technologies deployed to better manage and utilize information and knowledge slowly evolved over the course of several decades. With imaging came the realization that information beyond structured data could be manipulated and accessed at the speed of the computer – a machine that was allowing us to create information at unprecedented rates. Text retrieval demonstrated a technology approach to discover/learn from explicit knowledge sources via a content-relevant front end. Document management ushered in approaches to managing entire collections of explicit knowledge sources. Workflow provided not only control over business processes, but also the development of a new body of knowledge – dynamic metrics regarding performance. It is no coincidence, however, that the advent of Internet and intranet technology immediately precedes the technology emergence of knowledge management. The Internet and corporate counterparts, intranets, suddenly thrust upon the corporate world – from manager to employee – the reality of information management. Infoglut became a universal well-understood and shared challenge. Technology vendors scrambled to re-purpose existing tools and create new tools to address the issues of mining value out of existing knowledge resources. This movement, coupled with the growing intellectual focus on knowledge management and the value of intellectual capital, were collectively responsible for the sudden and immediate direct business focus on knowledge management.

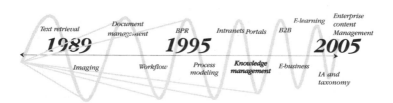

Fig. 3.1   Technology timeline.

As outlined in the Introduction, and illustrated in the timeline, the technology fervor regarding knowledge management waned rather quickly. It gave way to the next technology-promised panaceas, including B2B, portals, e-learning enterprise content management. Information architectures and Taxonomies. These are in reality tactical manifestations of knowledge management from a technology standpoint.

Knowledge management continues to be the subject of adamant debate and evolving theory in the business word. Knowledge management-related technology evolves under many names – targeted applications of specific functionality fine-tuned to address specific business institutions. The technology application of knowledge learning is the focus of the next chapter.

KEY LEARNING POINTS

» Outgrowth of an educated workforce starting in the 1950s.

» The European and Asian influences in the 1950s and 1960s.

» Identification of the knowledge worker by Peter Drucker in 1959.

» Identification of explicit and tacit knowledge by Polanyi in 1966.

» Peters and Waterman identify corporate best practices in 1982.

» Paul Strassmann pioneers the concept of information and knowledge assets in 1985.

» Hammer and Champy introduce the corporate world to the idea of reengineering in 1992.

» Knowledge management reacts years later as a more constant and permanent form of reengineering.

» Leif Edvinsson puts knowledge management on the corporate books in 1994.

» Nonaka introduces the world to "organizational knowledge creation" in 1995.

» The rise and fall of knowledge management in the late 1990s.

» The technology timeline and the practical applications of knowledge management.

04

The E-Dimension of Knowledge Management

Clearly, knowledge management is not about technology. But, technology has heightened the need for, and powers of, knowledge management. Practical technology approaches to knowledge management include:

- » personal profiling;
- » categorization/taxonomy;
- » visualization of knowledge;
- » search and retrieval;
- » agents;
- » workflow;
- » decision-support; and
- » the portal as a killer application.

"The new source of power is not money in the hands of a few but information in the hands of many."

John Naisbitt, author of MegaTrends

Clearly, knowledge management is not about technology. But, as discussed in Chapter 3, technology has played a role in heightening awareness of knowledge management, and in facilitating knowledge management practices in the corporation. No amount of technology can make up for a corporation whose mission and culture do not recognize and support knowledge sharing practices and investments in intellectual capital and innovation practices. But, given the advances made in technology that can affect and augment these practices and cultures, no knowledge management strategy is complete without a technology component.

Furthermore, technology, namely the Internet and intranets, sparked a wide-scale interest in the need for knowledge management. The sudden availability of a universal platform that provided simplified access to entire collections of explicit knowledge was a wake-up call to technicians and businessmen alike. To this day, technology is evolving to provide means for people to capture and store knowledge, broker sources of knowledge, and leverage knowledge in business settings (read knowledge management).

Fig. 4.1   Application of technology to knowledge management.

Fig. 4.1 illustrates how commonly used technologies form part of a knowledge management solution. Note that all the technologies are positioned on the explicit side of the diagram, while the solutions listed on the tacit side are all human-based. The application of technology to knowledge management is best understood when mapped to the knowledge management applications introduced and defined in Chapter 2. Technology should be tactically applied, not universally distributed. Technology will not replace the value of, and need for, face-to-face synchronous communication with regards to tacit knowledge, but technology can assist in brokering the owners of tacit knowledge and facilitating the creation of people-based networks.

Technologies for intermediation

A range of technologies can facilitate intermediation. These technologies are especially valuable for organizations that are highly distributed geographically and therefore less likely to encounter face-to-face or synchronous communication in the normal course of interaction among knowledge workers.

In support of the need for personal communication, intranets, instant messaging, online collaboration, e-mail and groupware applications can serve as meeting-places for establishing contact between knowledge seekers and knowledge providers. At a more powerful level, personal profiling systems can create online dossiers of individuals (i.e. tracking who they are, what projects they have worked on, search habits, what documents they have authored, edited, read, etc.). Subsequently, in response to a user query, these intermediation tools can provide the name and contact information for probable owners of relevant insight (i.e. tacit knowledge) on the subject of the query.

Technologies for externalization

The advent of the Web proved that the capturing and storage of knowledge sources was not as straightforward as one might have believed. Volumes of knowledge sources require intelligent approaches to categorization and navigation. Knowledge cannot be simply stored. To be effective it must be put into context.

Consider the complexity of creating and maintaining hypertext-linked World Wide Web documents, compared to a word processing file, and the required level of control becomes evident. Links should accurately denote the obvious and covert ties between separate forms of information to portray the knowledge value that comes from information in context.

Intelligent inventory systems that catalog knowledge both as it is needed and as it is encountered (i.e. entered) are required. The approach used must be dynamic. We are not categorizing information that can be stored in predefined categories and standard hierarchies, but knowledge that is changing continuously. Knowledge-based externalization technology reassesses the relationship of each body of knowledge with every other body of knowledge and maintains an ontology or taxonomy for the knowledge collection.

Visualization tools provide a graphical front end to these knowledge collections, illustrating the availability of the bodies of knowledge and their dependencies. These can be navigated to facilitate a knowledge discovery process.

Technologies for internalization

While externalization provides a view into the myriad connections it contains, internalization allows users to impose their perspective into the knowledge base and succinctly pluck out the relevant bodies of knowledge. Internalization technology is perhaps the oldest among the knowledge management tools, with its roots in simple search and retrieval engines. But, within the realm of knowledge management, the tools of internalization represent functionality that goes beyond simple word searches, to include functionality such as conceptual retrieval tools.

Technologies for cognition

Up until now, we have differentiated information from knowledge through the need for linkages and intelligence, or putting the information in context. However, both the links and the information need to follow certain rules in order to convey knowledge. This is the role of cognition tools.

Consider a salesperson that accesses a knowledge base to assess the buying habits of a competitor's customer. Numerous documents collected over time reflect prior sales opportunities with the prospect and the history of wins and losses. The history is linked to descriptive information about the prospect's business plans, markets, and strategy. These in turn may be linked to recent market activities that indicate the prospect's success in tapping new opportunities. All of this is important information. Yet, can the salesperson readily infer why the prospect might buy from his company, given the current circumstances in the market? With enough time and resources, perhaps.

An alternative would be to bundle certain analytical tools along with the knowledge. A simulation tool could create market profiles based on the current demand for the prospect's products. This tool could create the basis for a business case to buy from the salesperson's company rather than a competitor, perhaps due to an increased ability of the salesperson's company to deliver key support in an area of critical importance to the prospect's current market.

Most knowledge management cognition tools today are vertically focused. Decision support trees and case management and decision support tools are more easily created when focused on a finite problem, such as call centers, and sales force automation.

Finally, consider leveraging the powers of a workflow or BPM system as a cognition tool. These are tools that provide a means to automate the logic of business processes and execute that process repetitively. The focus of workflow is to ensure process integrity and decrease process time. Vicariously, however, these workflow tools also create audit trails, or histories of the business processes they automate.

Over time, these audit trails represent a body of knowledge regarding how different stimuli affect the business process (e.g. does the process move more readily when certain customers are involved, certain employees are involved, at certain times of the day, etc.). While this information is captured in the audit trail, it remains dormant in most products. By integrating investigative/analysis tools, the smart manager can unleash the knowledge within these audit trails, and possibly create automated decisions (cognition at its highest form) by having the workflow system alter process logic based on trends it recognizes.

KILLER APPLICATION NO. 1 – THE PORTAL

Portal technology is listed at every level of the knowledge application diagram. Emanating circa 1999, portals garnered much attention, more than virtually any other Internet technology over the past five years. Why?

As mentioned earlier, the rise of Internet technology resulted in a common frustrating experience for nearly everyone using the Web. From home users to knowledge workers, interaction with the computer environment rarely involves a single information resource. Even the simplest searches on the Web typically result in myriad references to myriad sources of data, processes, and people. In response, companies such as Yahoo! delivered integrated, categorized and personalized front ends to the Internet – portals. Corporate portals quickly followed on the heels of this technology approach, providing similar functionality and control over the organization's collective knowledge base.

From the point of view of the information work now driving business success, the portal is primarily a tool for accelerating and supporting knowledge and innovation processes. Companies deploy portals to combat the negative challenges of overabundance of information, discontinuity in the work environment, and disorganization in the computer systems' infrastructure.

The ideal habitat for the application of corporate portals it is at the intersection of the front and back office. This "middle office" operations space is best defined by the role and function of knowledge workers who constitute the linkage mechanism(s) between front office and back office information systems and processes. In its ability to coordinate the many information streams, people, and knowledge that create sound business practices, middle office work tends to have a direct and pivotal impact on maximizing profit, minimizing risk, and fostering innovation. Simply put, it is where organizations ultimately fail or succeed.

To provide a simplistic expansion on these definitions: back office functions focus on cost management and front office functions focus on revenue enhancement. While front and back office functions (from an information systems standpoint) have reached a stage of relative equilibrium and parity across most industries (thanks to extensive enterprise applications deployment encompassing common structured transactions), middle office workers live in a dynamic, unpredictable, and still largely manual work-world. Application of technology here has a payback that is measured in orders of magnitude.

Viewing the function of the middle office in the context of the knowledge chain (see Chapter 2 for more detail) makes clear that, as demand and fulfillment processes increasingly run on multiple tracks through a single individual (i.e. the middle office worker), there is increasing need to provide automation support to enhance that worker's performance. Consider, for example, the transformation going on today in the scope of the role of the customer service representative. No longer viewed as an afterthought function needed to deal with the consequences of customer confusion or process quality breakdowns, the service representative now occupies a middle office position addressing an increasingly broad set of customer needs. In forward-thinking companies, this role is now as much involved in market analysis and sales as it is in customer problem resolution.

The role of corporate portals in the middle office is to offer a tool that will automate the "linkage" aspect of the work environment. The great attraction to the idea of portals is based on their ability to create a "single point of access," which integrates, within one interface, the unstructured content of knowledge work with information from the wide variety of ERP, document, and CRM systems. This interface has the potential to render obsolete the contemporary standard of Windows-based application metaphors we use today.

It is important to establish that the portal is not a thing, but an application of a broad set of technologies following a very customized information design. The corporate portal design derives from the unique business and information landscape of the individual organization.

Because of the important role that both existing corporate information systems and external information sources play in supporting an organization's knowledge workers, and because the principal charter of the portal is to provide a single point of access to all information sources, the portal must take on the unprecedented role of universal integration mechanism. At the same time, since every individual's professional (and personal) information needs are different, the portal takes on the unprecedented role of delivering a personalized, function-centered desktop. Given the complexity of these challenges, portal implementations require a substantial set of architectural elements and components, as illustrated in Fig. 4.2 and in the following discussion.

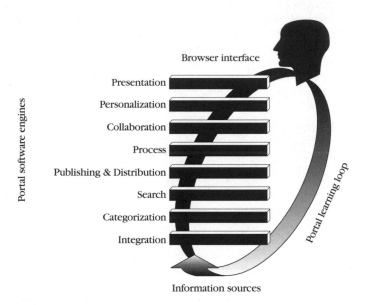

Fig. 4.2 Portal software architecture components.

Integration

The integration facility provides the foundation function of accessing information from the wide range of internal and external information sources and making them available for display at the portal. It allows a knowledge base of tacit and explicit sources, from image to video, to function as one virtual repository.

Categorization

The categorization facility implements the organization-specific taxonomy that helps contextualize portal information to support rapid recognition and productive use. This is a direct tie to the knowledge application of externalization.

Search

The search component provides a centralized facility for pinpoint access to specific information items. An effective search offering should include comprehensive indexing, metadata access, full-text access, and concept-based search. It should also support single point of access by providing a single point of search, i.e. the issuance of a single query results in relevant knowledge from multiple repositories, properly contextualized and ranked in a single result set.

Publishing and distribution

This functionality moves the portal beyond a research environment and into an interactive one. It supports content creation, authorization, and posting to the portal and should ensure accuracy, authentication, and timeliness.

Process support

Because the focus of the portal should include e-business management, process support is a critical foundation element. Process automation applications route documents and forms, receive and respond to intermediate "state changes" in a business process (e.g. credit approval messages from authorization systems, initiate transactions, trigger events in invoicing, inventory, or distribution systems), and provide audit and housekeeping services to monitor predefined process flows.

Collaboration

Collaboration enables community and expands the role of the corporate portal to a new forum for organizational interactions: between employees and among employees, customers, partners, and other stakeholders. Both synchronous (chat forums) and asynchronous communications (e.g. threaded discussions, team rooms that centrally collect documents, work schedules and so on for a particular team) can be available.

Personalization

The personalization facility is a critical ingredient in productivity enhancement and effective individual information management. It supports the "My!" view of the knowledge base popularized by the Internet portal environments. The "My!" facility gives the portal interface a new value proposition at two levels: users can select categories or channels of content for display in their view; and users can control the placement and prominence of the content items they require. Corporate portal applications should also provide the ability to personalize portal content by centralizing, managing, and prioritizing the delivery of information on a job-function or interest basis.

Presentation

Portals must integrate information display, context and ease of use at the same time. Today, most users accept the hierarchical foldering metaphor, although newer alternatives, in richer media and a fuller communications range (e.g. PDAs and cell phones), are gaining popularity.

Learning loops

The portal learning loop differs from the other architectural elements in that it is not concerned with a specific aspect of information management, but in the ongoing effectiveness of the portal itself. The learning loop is an application of knowledge management itself, rather than an application for knowledge management. The learning loop dynamically collects and analyzes the collective wisdom innate in the interaction between user and portal. These metrics are used to detect and adjust to ongoing changes in user information needs in Internet time. It can affect changes in any of the other layers of portal functionality without directly involving the user. The knowledge environment adapts to the user's evolving needs.

BEST PRACTICES IN KM
The World Bank

Created in 1944, and owned by 1832 member countries, the World Bank is an international financial institution and development agency. Recently, the bank repositioned its strategy to directly address the issue of poverty in the global community. As part of that effort, in 1996, the then president of the bank, James Wolfensohn, began a strategic knowledge management initiative throughout the bank. Wolfensohn believed that the bank's involvement with governments, institutions and development projects around the world created a valuable knowledge base. He stated: "To capture this potential we need to invest in the necessary systems that will enhance our ability to gather development information and experience and share it with our clients. We need to become, in effect, the 'Knowledge Bank'."

A task force was formed to make this vision a reality. By Fall 1996, the bank was ready to roll out its first knowledge network: EKMS – the Education Knowledge Management System. EKMS served approximately 300 users from the bank's education sector. EKMS facilitates collaboration, knowledge sharing and discovery of areas to be addressed. The EKMS staff identify best practices and provide training for education staff. Within EKMS, nine separate focus groups were formed, targeted at specific educational issues such as education technology, effective schools and teachers, and the economics of education. EKMS supports a Website that provides worldwide access to documented best practices, tools, creative ideas, key readings, links to related Websites and bibliographical information. Thus an online community is being propagated. By the end of 1998, there were over 100 theme-based communities in place. The bank learned that to be successful, the communities each needed a facilitator who is somewhat familiar with the subject matter of focus, has good team-building skills, and good communication skills. This person is also responsible for keeping Web content current.

Additionally, a manned help desk is provided that will answer specific questions. A log of all questions and answers is maintained and provided as yet another resource. The logs are examined, looking for trends. Where arising knowledge needs are seen, specific projects are spun off to fill that information need and add the research to the online library.

Simultaneously, the bank's IT staff was working to create a technology backbone to support this effort. This team started by looking at a legacy of multiple disparate systems. The knowledge management infrastructure used to tie the legacy together is a suite of Lotus Notes tools and Website platforms.

The World Bank still considers its knowledge management initiative in its infancy, and views cultural resistance as the biggest hurdle yet to be fully scaled. Despite this, a poll of bank employees found that 90 percent find the results to date useful or very useful; 70 percent found that EKMS made their work more effective. A good example of the system's usefulness is when a staff member in Nepal needed insight on implementation plan models to help clients in the Nepalese Ministry of Education prepare for the next phase of a primary education project. Using the EKMS system, the staff member located not only a generic implementation plan, but also contacts in Hungary and Turkey with best practices experiences in rolling out similar education projects.

KEY LEARNING POINTS

» The effect of infoglut on the need for knowledge management.
» Technology enablers to a knowledge management practice:
  » personal profiling;
  » categorization;
  » visualization of knowledge;
  » search and retrieval;
  » agents;
  » workflow and e-process; and
  » decision support.
» The portal as knowledge management killer application.
» Best practices in knowledge management:
  » case study of the World Bank.

05

The Global Dimension of Knowledge Management

Knowledge management is about the complete and open sharing of knowledge across all boundaries, whether departmental, corporate or regional. By its very definition it elicits global cooperation. The examination of basic knowledge management practices at the global level includes:

» the effect of the World Wide Web on knowledge management;
» global knowledge communities; and
» global knowledge markets.

"The real questions are how do we stay connected? How do we share knowledge? How do we function any time, anywhere, no matter what?"

Robert Buckman, former CEO of Buckman Laboratories and knowledge management zealot

There is nothing localized about knowledge and knowledge management. Indeed, in its purest sense, knowledge management is about the complete and open sharing of knowledge. The evolution of knowledge management itself has served as a quintessential melting pot. Consider where pivotal input regarding knowledge management and the identification of the value of intellectual capital has come from: Sveiby and Erickson from Sweden; Itami and Nonaka from Japan; Thomas Stewart and Paul Romer from the USA; and Hubert St Onge and Dr Nick Bontis from Canada (see Chapter 3 for more detail on the evolution of knowledge management).

Knowledge knows no cerebral boundaries and, with the advent of the Web, it knows no physical limits. In Chapter 4 we explored the ways in which the advent of the Web affected the usage and adoption of knowledge management. One issue was not yet discussed, and that is the subject of this chapter, globalization. There was a Nortel Networks commercial on television. It highlighted real-time sharing of news and information around the globe. The closing of the commercial is highlighted in background by the singing of lyrics from a Beatles song: "Come together, right now, over me." Indeed, communities of practice can assemble using state-of-the-art telecommunications and the Web with unprecedented ease today. Knowledge management is the bedrock to this proposition. Formalized approaches to amassing bodies of explicit knowledge, and the tracking and identification of tacit knowledge owners, creates a resource that can be well tapped in a global/Internet environment. Today, knowledge communities and knowledge markets exist across the globe, which is in no small way due to the availability of a global infrastructure.

But, it is not just the availability of a global infrastructure that has resulted in the formation of global knowledge markets and knowledge communities. The growing culture of the global population advances this cause as well. Consider the impetus for knowledge management (see Chapter 3). Clearly, WWII was a turning point in global history in many ways. A greatly educated workforce emerged. Great scientific advancements were made. As a result of the war, the world's population has taken many great strides to improve global conditions and global harmony on several fronts. For example, the United Nations was conceived as a forum to promote political exchange and advocate political stability. The International Monetary Fund and the World Bank were founded to promote the flow of financial capital globally. Knowledge sharing and the flow of intellectual capital has been perhaps a bit slower in developing official bodies for self-promotion. But it has been coming nonetheless.

We can trace the roots of the World Wide Web back to Vannevar Bush, science advisor to President Roosevelt during WWII. At the end of the war, Bush wrote an article ('As We May Think,' *Atlantic Monthly*, July 1945) in which he espoused the need for a global infrastructure in order to link the world's know-how. He felt that the knowledge amassed by the world scientific community in an effort to win the war would be lost in vain if it could not be adequately shared, linked, made assessable and re-purposed. His invention of the memex (MEMory EXtender) was the embryo of today's Internet. The Internet is known as the World Wide Web – not a European Web, or an American Web, or even an Asian Web, but a *World* Wide Web. Its premise is indeed to link the world of knowledge, as Bush envisioned.

Similar to the forming of the UN and IMF, in 1998 (a long time coming) the GKII (Global Knowledge Innovation Infrastructure) was formed and met for the first time. Although it has yet to reach the notoriety and clout of the IMF or UN, it is a beginning. Its mission, to ensure that knowledge flows globally.

So, the infrastructure and global culture are ripe for global knowledge sharing. What have we done to seize these opportunities? Global knowledge management has taken two forms thus far: knowledge communities and global knowledge markets.

GLOBAL KNOWLEDGE COMMUNITIES

Global knowledge communities can be created in an intra-organizational manner. Co-workers are now empowered to share and collaborate beyond their physical boundaries. I recently had the opportunity to assist in the design of a knowledge management practice for one of the big five consulting firms. When we started our design process with a definition of core goals (for more information about core goals and their role in solution design, see Chapter 10), goal one emerged as facilitated collaboration – to leverage the organization's talent, experience and know-how (i.e. intellectual capital) around the world. Nothing precluded this company from doing this before, nothing culturally, that is. But technology, time and distance stood in their way. A properly designed knowledge management system that employs personal profiling, agents and search/internalization tools, which were exercised across the firm's many local repositories, enabled rapid worldwide collaboration. (See Chapters 4 and 6 for more information about these knowledge management technologies.) Not only is there anticipation of increased success in winning proposals and faster turnarounds on proposals and reports, but travel costs, a major expense for this global services company, were projected to be cut by as much as 25 percent.

Similar work with a global metals company resulted in a system that made available over the corporate intranet best practices and lessons learned in plants around the world: several US sites, Brazil, Jamaica, Spain, Italy, and Australia. Physical location challenges and local issues were surmounted via a global knowledge community practice.

These examples are indicative of the pressures that organizations feel today. Global economies, global branding, and global workforces are mandating that companies look at leveraging their global intellectual capital. It is difficult for me to recall a client engagement in the last three years that did not address this issue in some capacity. Work with pharmaceutical companies, for example, almost immediately turns to issues regarding global research coordination, global filing/protection of intellectual capital (e.g. patents and trademarks) and coordinated global marketing. Perhaps for centuries we have instinctively recognized that specialized knowledge can exist in global pockets. We often speak of German engineering, American ingenuity and Asian productivity. Global knowledge communities offer a way to create a sum greater than its parts by facilitating and promoting coordination and collaboration among these. In fact, one might argue that without practical and effective means to establish global knowledge practices, the recent emergence of offshoring and outsourcing would not have been possible.

(It should be noted that cultural issues typically present major challenges to global knowledge communities, both in terms of corporate culture and regional/societal culture. Learn more about these challenges and ways to address them in Chapter 6.)

Global knowledge communities have emerged in intercorporation forums as well. This is the outsourcing model that is growing in popularity. But beyond that, there are also vortals (portals developed and organized by an entire vertical industry) that educate the corporate global community as to the value and leverage in knowledge sharing across competitors, suppliers, customers and partners in a vertical market space. A prime example of this is Covisint, the automotive vortal formed by Daimler-Chrysler, Ford and General Motors. Though primarily focused on streamlined procurement and production, this vortal, and others like it, involve the exchange of knowledge, a trend that will continue. Such systems have given rise to the premise of the knowledge market.

GLOBAL KNOWLEDGE MARKETS

On a parallel route to the concept of the vortal, the concept of the knowledge markets has emerged. Clearly, this knowledge practice is steeped in the proposition that intellectual capital has real value. Because they were born on the Internet, these markets are by their very nature globally scoped and deployed.

Global knowledge markets are a form of portal (See Chapter 4 for more details on portals) that match the needs of a knowledge seeker with resources of potential knowledge providers and subsequently enable a knowledge transaction. The nature of the transaction may be financial, a barter or complimentary. Some exchanges facilitate the transference of explicit (recorded) knowledge. Others broker exchange of tacit knowledge. Hybrid exchanges also exist. All have their place. In much the same way that B2B exchanges facilitate the ease in which buyers and sellers meet to conduct transactions over the Internet, knowledge markets enable opportunities for knowledge providers and knowledge seekers to conduct transactions that, without the knowledge market, would have otherwise been difficult at best, likely impossible.

Increased market exposure for owners of knowledge products, centralized collections of like knowledge products, and acceptable pricing models for valuing the knowledge product increase the quality and quantity of knowledge products through the dynamics of open competition. Knowledge markets expedite the discovery of knowledge globally and, through the Web, turn that into a business proposition.

Global knowledge markets manifest under three business models: knowledge auctions, question and answer, and intellectual property exchanges.

Knowledge auction markets function under a loosely defined community of buyers and sellers, similar to online product auction sites popularized by sites such as eBay. Buyers and sellers partake in an ad hoc, dynamic, pricing-based demand environment. Knowledge is both offered and requested, along with the price the consumer is willing to pay for the desired information and the suggested selling price from the supplier. Pricing for knowledge may be bid-up as the demand increases or may fall if the information is topical or if the provider is rated poorly. Knowledge is immediately available for downloading once a price is agreed upon. An example of a knowledge auction market is www.knexa.com.

A lack of brand recognition in e-knowledge markets has resulted in the venture capitalist (VC) syndrome of "What is it?" Although the concept of a knowledge exchange is a relatively new idea, we are witnessing rapid growth in terms of number of Websites, variations of services offered and how knowledge is exchanged. This will surely help VCs in understanding the potential of knowledge markets. Without the support of significant capital, many knowledge markets are starting small and slowly building brand recognition, which, over time, will result in an increase in demand, with an increase in prices to follow.

Question and answer-based knowledge markets are best utilized for the exchange of tacit expertise. In this model, prices are fixed by the knowledge holder and based on a cost per minute for a live exchange of information facilitated by the hosting site through a telephone connection. Examples of question and answer markets include www.keen.com and www.infomarkets.com.

Intellectual property knowledge exchanges were created to allow corporations to market their intellectual property (e.g. patents, trade secrets and trademarks) on the global market. Under this model, corporations are finding new avenues from which to gather revenue from their intellectual property. Patents that have not been leveraged by the patent owner are a particularly powerful new way to get value from an untapped source of intellectual property. Sellers of such intellectual property seek out and offer knowledge to non-competing industries where the knowledge can be applied in innovative ways, specific to their industry, and not within the purview of the knowledge owner. This is the quintessential example of the promise of knowledge management – sharing knowledge and, as a result, re-purposing it in innovate ways. Examples of intellectual property exchanges include www.yet2.com and www.techex.com.

Knowledge markets – at what price?

Perhaps the biggest challenge that global knowledge markets face today is establishing value. Knowledge as a commercial commodity is a new concept and, as such, it is difficult to determine how to place value on it. Pushing this model onto the global economy only furthers the challenge. Is knowledge of a particular type worth more based on where the buyer is geographically located? Knowledge auctions, in theory, will permit the natural economic forces of supply and demand to determine pricing. But pricing is only one of the areas that knowledge markets are forcing the global community to face. Others include reliability of information, liability and ownership. These and other issues form the subject of Chapter 6.

BEST PRACTICE IN KM

Dow Chemical

Most people think of Dow Chemical Co. as a manufacturer of chemical, agricultural and plastic products. But Dow considers itself primarily a research and development company – it is correct for honing in on its core competency, rather than its products. For years, however, Dow minimally leveraged the fruits of its R&D practice. That situation began to change in 1993 when the company implemented a knowledge management program to help increase the value of its patent information.

By the mid-1990s Dow provided a standard desktop for virtually all of its employees. Corporate intranets, on which an array of information was posted, were constructed. But internalization functionality was lacking. Users were never sure if they had the "best" sources of knowledge at any given time. Available information was doubling every 18 months. Different groups used different knowledge bases. To resolve these problems, Dow took the next step in its KM program in January 2000.

An 11-member executive team was formed to build a five-year knowledge management plan. This team created the position of information steward, an individual to preside over the knowledge sharing practice of each Dow business group. The stewards evangelize and implement the company's knowledge management efforts, getting documents under control and certifying each document's authenticity and value. Stewards educate their unit members on the values of KM and promote knowledge sharing by explaining how available knowledge management technologies can accelerate business strategies and help the units achieve their individual goals.

In this manner, knowledge management was not seen as something dictated from on high, but developed at a grass-roots level. Each unit, via its steward, created its own policies and procedures with regards to knowledge management. However, to ensure corporate knowledge sharing, as applicable, the unit stewards also report into the Knowledge Management Resource Center, an executive centralized group. The role of the center is to establish broad KM initiatives and provide assistance to the stewards with application and roll out. The Knowledge Management Program Office, a centralized team based in the IT department, also provides the stewards with technical assistance. Most importantly, the stewards, who are spread across the USA and Europe, meet as a committee in person for a three-day retreat each quarter, hold teleconferences every six weeks, and routinely communicate informally through e-mail. In this manner they have created their own knowledge sharing practice. This enables them to share steward-based best practices, and look for knowledge sharing opportunities between their respective units.

Dow has set its sights on many benefits from this practice. One is decreasing the duplication of information. Success has come in many ways in different units. For example, the epoxy products and polyurethane unit instituted committees that review and keep current its intranet sites, organize technical information to facilitate discovery, and have implemented search and collaboration tools. The performance chemicals unit has reportedly saved millions of dollars through improved customer service, made possible by better and accessible documentation.

Through this effort, Dow estimates to have saved $125 million since 1993. More importantly, early on in the project, Dow management realized that intellectual capital beyond patents was lying dormant and underused within the company. Dow planning to put their knowledge practice under a portal application, figuring that if money could be saved by better handling patents, they could save even more if they better manage "soft" intellectual capital assets.

KEY LEARNING POINTS

» The effect of the World Wide Web on knowledge management.
» Global knowledge communities:
  » vortals.
» Global knowledge exchanges:
» Outsourcing & offshoring
  » knowledge auction markets;
  » question and answer-based markets;
  » intellectual property knowledge markets; and
  » pricing intellectual property in a global deployment.

06

The State of the Art of Knowledge Management

Knowledge management is a subject ripe for debate and many of the current burning issues are examined here, including the following.

» ROI – how to justify investments in knowledge management.
» Knowledge and leadership – is a CKO necessary?
» Culture – from corporate cultures to regional cultures, how important are these issues and how should they be handled?
» Beyond the four walls – sharing knowledge in an intercorporate environment.
» Trust and liability – vulnerability in knowledge sharing.
» Ownership of knowledge.
» Organization – making sense of infoglut.
» Content management, knowbots and videography.
» Free agency.

"When knowledge stops evolving it turns into opinion or dogma."
Thomas Davenport and Larry Prusak

Knowledge management is a subject ripe for debate. The very premise of knowledge management is that we grow by continuously challenging what we know and how we apply it. As Davenport and Prusak point out, if knowledge is not allowed to evolve, it morphs into opinion. Is it any wonder, then, that in both the academic and business communities, debates regarding knowledge management thrive?

As highlighted throughout this title, knowledge management has been evolving for several decades, and it has caused many changes in financial accounting and business practice, let alone corporate culture. It has been, and will continue to be, a highly complex issue linked to many sub-issues, each equally complex in their own right: corporate culture; copyright, security and knowledge ownership; valuation of intellectual capital; evolving business models and practices; job descriptions; employee incentivization; and leadership styles. It is part art and part science. On these issues, we have only begun to scratch the surface. New technologies will come and go. New approaches to establishing businesses will rise and fall (witness the recent fall of dot-com mania to dot-bomb reality). But through all of these, knowledge management will linger, and be found at the heart of many.

What are the current hot topics regarding knowledge management? What are the latest technology trends that affect it? What issues are currently major points of contention for the business manager and knowledge worker? Among the most turbulent are the following.

» ROI (return on investment) – how to justify investments in knowledge management.
» Knowledge and leadership – is a CKO necessary?
» Culture – from corporate cultures to regional cultures, how important are these issues and how should they be handled?
» Beyond the four walls – sharing knowledge in an intercorporate environment.
» Trust and liability – vulnerability in knowledge sharing.
» Ownership of knowledge.
» Organization – making sense of infoglut.

» Content management, knowbots and videography.
» Free agency.

KNOWLEDGE MANAGEMENT – IS IT WORTH IT?

The question of evaluating the merits of knowledge management to the organization is one of particular interest of late, given the current state of the economy. Knowledge management is not supported simply with a management vision – as it was just a year ago. Today, CEOs and CFOs are asking for hard dollar returns. There are three parts to this answer.

To satisfy the fiscal reality needs of today's management, ask management to give you the hot spots or metrics by which they wish to see an ROI. Why would they invest not only in knowledge management, but any information-handling technology? What issues do they feel need to be addressed to ensure the solvency and competitiveness of the organization? Is time-to-market a major factor in how they define success? Or is the rate of producing new product ideas? Is minimizing resource costs while scaling production up a major concern? Is minimizing rework a major issue? Is lack of consistency jeopardizing customer satisfaction or putting the organization at risk? No ROI on knowledge management can begin until these business goals are defined.

Simultaneously, an assessment of the current state of knowledge management within the firm and a determination of the propensity of the organization to be knowledge driven must be made (see Chapter 10 to learn more about knowledge audits and the audit process).

The analysis of these findings should be viewed in light of the critical success factors. It is only in the juxtaposition of these two variables that a valid ROI can be constructed. For example, management within a major US federal lobbying group that I worked with expressed the need to increase productivity with existing staff. Business had to grow without increasing personnel costs. Among the findings in their audit was realization that many knowledge workers exerted approximately 20 percent of their time looking for precedent, existing expertise in house, and general knowledge external to the organization. It was also found that it took approximately five years for an employee to become proficient in identifying and leveraging existing in-house resources with any degree of efficiency. By augmenting existing intranet technology within the origination, we demonstrated a return of more than half the time required to research issues and a virtual elimination in employee acclamation. This was time returned to staff, so to speak, which could be used in production and innovation tasks versus discovery. This had a huge impact on management's understanding of how knowledge management would provide real dollar value to the organization.

In literally every case where I have conducted an audit, gems such as this have been uncovered. It is uncanny how much opportunity exists in organizations to maximize existing resources and investments. The trick is to determine the reality of what users face each day in every facet of their jobs, and to determine how issues can be reconciled or leveraged in order to support management's success factors.

Lastly, as practicioner/pundits such as Gordon Petrash and Leif Edvinsson have taught us, value can be found in the products of knowledge management – intellectual capital – itself. As companies become increasingly dependent on their internal knowledge for their success and growth, so their value is shifting from physical assets to the intangible assets of knowledge.

Measuring this "intellectual capital" is, however, no easy task. Intellectual capital can include such diverse and loosely defined resources as employees' knowledge and skills, customer relationships, employee motivation, and knowledge-supporting infrastructures. Nevertheless, some well-known examples such as Swedish insurer Skandia AFS have made significant inroads into this field. As Edvinsson put it, it is "better to be roughly right than precisely wrong." Much talk has surrounded this new form of capital, which is commonly divided into three categories: intellectual capital, customer capital, and structural capital (see Chapter 8 for definitions of each of these forms of capital).

The total of these three forms of capital is often considered to be the difference in value from book value to market value. However, even this is short sighted since market value may suffer in the short term while intellectual capital is converted to structural capital and new innovations are being built.

Perhaps the easiest way to understand the value of these forms of capital in any organization is to look at how they are measured within the knowledge chain as return on time (ROT) (see Chapter 2 for more details on the knowledge chain).

The following equation assesses how innovative an organization is by measuring its ability to sustain innovation over a period of time: the higher the ROT, the more innovative and competitive the organization.

ROT = [(% of profit/100) × (sustained years/number of years)]

For example, a company that for the past five years has derived 50 percent of its profit for each year from products that have been introduced in that same year has an ROT of 2.5. Not bad. However, a company that for ten years has derived 100 percent of its yearly profit from product introduced in the last three years would have an ROT of 3.3. Even better.

This sort of simple analysis masks the complexity of multiple product lines and varying profit contributions by each line. In fact, a complete ROT analysis must look at the life cycle and contribution of every product over the time period being measured. However, even a simple analysis of available public data provides a clear sense for where your organization stands in its industry relative to its competitors. The main thing to keep in mind about ROT is that it is a relative measure. There is no absolute measure. As with any other measure of return (return on investment, internal rate of return, return on assets, etc.) you need only do better than your competitors in your market's context to be successful.

KNOWLEDGE AND LEADERSHIP – IS A CKO NECESSARY?

In a study done for *KM Magazine* in May 2001, it was found that a pivotal issue in migrating to a knowledge strategy is the creation of a culture to support trust and collaboration. Clearly, if knowledge is to permeate your organization, redefine the manner in which value is measured, change the way in which individuals approach their work, and alter corporate culture forever, there must be an internal champion to lead the knowledge cause. Since Leif Edvinsson was titled the first Chief Knowledge Officer (CKO), speculation has waged as to what form of leader is necessary and what level of authority that leader needs to be effective.

It can be argued that knowledge leadership is not new. Managing the knowledge of a process is a requirement in any enterprise, even an enterprise of only one person. However, today, knowledge is not the proprietary property of a few craftspeople or executives working within the inner sanctum of an organization. Instead, it is a common property of virtually all workers. Add to this the transient nature of today's workforce, the need to quickly connect and mobilize geographically disbursed teams, and the highly technical nature of modern work and you have an immense demand for greater sophistication in the way knowledge is managed.

Although there are a number of organizations with CKOs in place, these are rare. Many other lesser-known titles and associated responsibilities are in use in organizations throughout the world to identify and characterize their knowledge leaders. You should consider each of these and determine the approach that is best for you and your organization. This is not a lesson in semantics. You will find that subtle but critical differences in style, value and approach are reflected in these various titles and characterizations. Although no taxonomy could possibly set forth all of the titles and responsibilities included under this moniker, the following are general categories you should consider.

» Knowledge engineer.
» Knowledge analyst.
» Knowledge manager.
» Chief knowledge officer.
» Knowledge steward.

Knowledge engineer

The knowledge engineer is a leader typically associated with an organization that is taking a very tactical/procedural approach to knowledge management. As the title infers, the knowledge engineer is responsible for converting explicit knowledge to instructions, programs systems and codified applications. The knowledge engineer reduces knowledge-based work to replicable procedures by codifying them. The principle challenge of this position is performing it without outgrowing it. Effectively, the better knowledge engineers codify knowledge, the harder it is for the organization to change when their environment demands it.

Knowledge analyst

This type of knowledge leader is a conduit to best practices. The knowledge analyst is responsible for collecting, organizing and disseminating knowledge, usually on demand. Knowledge analysts provide knowledge leadership by becoming walking repositories of best practices. The liability, of course, is that they can easily take all of the best practices with them if they leave. There is also a risk that these individuals become so valuable to the immediate constituency they serve that they are not able to move laterally to other parts of the organization where their skills are equally needed.

Knowledge manager

As the title infers, the knowledge manager is an overseer. This approach to leadership works best in organizations that believe knowledge will primarily be the responsibility of multiple individuals throughout the organization. The knowledge manager is responsible for coordinating the efforts of engineers, architects, and analysts. This position is most often required in large organizations in which the number of discrete knowledge sharing processes risk fragmentation and isolation and the knowledge manager provides the same level of coordination across these as a director of marketing may provide across a number of products. The risk in having knowledge managers is that fiefdoms may begin to form around the success of each manager's domain.

Chief knowledge officer (CKO)

This is a very traditional, hierarchical approach to the management of knowledge. The CKO is responsible for enterprise-wide coordination of all knowledge leadership and typically reports to, or is chartered by, the CEO. Although it would go to reason that the CKO be part of IT (perhaps reporting to the CIO) this is not often the case. The CKO is not tasked with the infrastructure technology but, rather, the practice of knowledge leadership. At present the role is almost always a solo performer with little, if any, staff and no immediate line-of-business responsibility. The principle liability of putting a CKO in place is doing it too early: the CKO is powerless before a culture of knowledge sharing, incentives, and the basic precepts of knowledge leadership have been acknowledged by the enterprise, or at least a significant portion of it.

Knowledge steward

The knowledge steward is similar to a knowledge manager. The steward thrives in organizations that do not view knowledge as a corporate resource that must be managed from the top down. This role is responsible for providing minimal but ongoing support to knowledge users in the form of expertise in the tools, practices and methods of knowledge leadership. The steward is in the most precarious and most opportunistic of positions. Usually he or she is an individual who has fallen into the role of helping others to better understand and leverage the power of new technologies and practices in managing knowledge.

Which of these roles is best suited for your organization? The principal determinants are the state of your organization's knowledge sharing, the level of sponsorship for knowledge leadership and the receptivity of its culture today.

When interviewing Thomas Brailsford at Hallmark Cards regarding why his organization avoided the use of a CKO, he offered this advise:

> "A CKO cannot manage knowledge. Knowledge exists with the workers; knowledge is inseparable from the people. Knowledge management is an oxymoron. You can't manage it. And that's one reason we wanted to stay away from knowledge management. We wanted leadership. We felt like leadership was much more appropriate than management. So we've concluded that you cannot separate knowledge creation from the people nor from their jobs. And that learning and acquiring knowledge is an actual by-product of, or is the essence of, a knowledge worker's profession. And so, that is a naturally occurring process throughout your organization. Rather than having a person who can bring all of that together, you need to have a culture, and an infrastructure that facilitates bringing all that stuff together."

Kent Greenes at BP, which has been widely publicized as a leader in knowledge-based initiatives due to its CEO's (John Browne) outspoken nature on the subject, describes the approach they use for knowledge leadership as developing an internal capacity in the individual business units:

> "I spend most of my time engaging the businesses and doing the awareness and stewarding and coaching. We don't do any bit of support unless there is a business champion that says I want to do

this, or we influence them or convince him or her to do it, and they own it. In fact, we take it so far as they have to demonstrate that advocacy if they want our help by putting their own business people in a role part-time to be the person who receives and internalizes what we do so that it becomes part of a sustainable capacity in their own team and the organization. So, our main approach is all about creating an internal capacity for this, not at the top, but within each business area. The response has been great. Right now, in our eighty business units, there are about one hundred people who are calling themselves knowledge managers, knowledge guardians, knowledge harvesters, or knowledge coordinators. It does not matter what they are called. When we engage them, we put it in their language and meet them where they are at.''

Dow Chemical takes a slightly different approach to knowledge leadership. According to Jim Allen of Dow Chemical:

''We do not have a CKO. If I had to guess, I don't think we will have a CKO. We have the human relations resources groups that have certain responsibilities for the development of competencies and how groups can better share and network. The other piece we have is intellectual asset management. Their job is limited to evaluation of intellectual assets and better practices for managing intellectual assets. We have the information systems folks, who are, as we move towards the information-sharing world, the road builders to a large extent. And then the individual business groups, by themselves, have the ultimate responsibility for their knowledge. Those individual core groups have certain competencies or their own business product process competencies. They have specific responsibilities for all their subject matter and knowledge management.''

The bottom line, stated once again, is that a knowledge leader of one type or another is a requisite of a successful knowledge initiative. However, you should not assume that the title CKO, and the role it connotes, is the best way to provide that leadership.

CULTURE – FROM CORPORATE CULTURES TO REGIONAL CULTURES, HOW IMPORTANT ARE THESE ISSUES AND HOW SHOULD THEY BE HANDLED?

''The greatest difficulty lies not in persuading people to accept new ideas, but in persuading them to abandon old ones.''

John Maynard Keynes

In a *Bulletpoint* (issue 51, May 1998) article, it was reported that 7 percent of polled managers expressed disappointment with their KM practices, based on culture as the biggest obstacle to effective KM. Some 7 years later, little has changed. Without exception, failed KM initiatives can almost always be linked back to an unsupportive culture. Clearly, cultures that subtly (or overtly) subvert the introduction of knowledge management can kill any hope of success, if not properly managed and changed. In Chapter 10 the concept of the knowledge audit is overviewed. A primary outcome of the audit is the identification of what the challenges within your particular organization are. But, while the specifics of each organization's challenges are unique, you must recognize that there are some basic universal challenges that will have to be confronted. What are these basic issues? We are speaking of building a community of knowledge sharers, the ownership of knowledge, and incentivization, each discussed below.

In order for the knowledge base to have value, it must be used by the entire organization. Anything short provides an incomplete picture of the organization's knowledge resources. This is not simply a matter of building an effective system, but creating and nurturing a knowledge sharing community within the organization. If there are no such communities, and no chance to create them, any attempts to propagate knowledge are futile.

In a lobbying organization for which I conducted a knowledge audit, we discovered that while senior management spoke frequently of knowledge sharing, their actions at committee meetings, corporate meetings and departmental memos stressed departmental rivalry. Budgets were an item of contention among departments – all vying for the same dollars. These ''untouted'' actions gave subliminal messages, but strong messages just the same. Inter-departmental collaboration and sharing were nearly unheard of. Users spoke of co-workers from other areas as "enemies" and questioned any inquisitive acts from the departments. There was no sense of community here. This became the main issue, which had to be reconciled before any investments in knowledge management systems could be justified.

In an aerospace company, users were frustrated by senior management who asked them to be innovative, but often publicly squashed the innovation. The lack of a clear corporate mission statement confused users. Good ideas would result in the production of new product (at best) but ultimately, rather than being congratulated, senior management often would announce the elimination of the product/plan because it was contrary to corporate mission and direction. However, no one knew what that mission was, and often saw it as a moving target and a weapon that could be used arbitrarily. But, unlike the lobbying group, users still felt a sense of community. They collectively agreed on what was wrong, and formed many informal support groups. This is actually not such a bad culture from a community standpoint. With minor changes to corporate vision and communication, the community culture could be focused on positive issues.

In one pharmaceutical company, a very strong community spirit was discovered. It existed on two planes, geographically and project-wise. The project communities were examples of groups with a common cause (i.e. to get a drug to market). When speaking of the corporation and co-workers, employees used words such as "family." This, coupled with a general atmosphere of openness throughout the organization, created a group dynamic that could be, and was, used as a starting point to build knowledge-based communities. The introduction of simple technology changes and process changes created a system in which employees could easily transfer lessons learned far and wide throughout the organization, not just in their own drug team.

Of course corporate culture can be compounded by regional cultures when deploying knowledge management in a global setting. But, the bottom line here is to have the "proper" corporate culture in place to manage and direct regional issues. For example, at an international metals company, regional differences, founded predominately in language, suppressed an otherwise positive corporate culture towards knowledge sharing. A strategic mandate that all business be conducted in English was not enough. Users acquiesced, but at sites where English was not the mother tongue, those less proficient in the language were reluctant to share knowledge as the translation process was too time consuming. Similarly, lessons learned were often difficult to appreciate when translation was done individually. Corporate culture was not strong enough to overcome the physical realities of regional languages. Simple changes to approaches to translation, fueled by an otherwise positive corporate culture, dramatically turned around the rate and quality of knowledge sharing.

Compare this to a pharmaceutical company in which language was not a difference, but regional "personality" was. Drug teams that spanned across the Atlantic, from the USA to the UK, shared a common language (of course some British might argue that the Americans do not really speak English). But users complained of opposing subtle differences in work style. Americans were characterized as "cowboys, who shoot first and then ask why," whereas the British were characterized as "over-thinkers who will ponder an issue for months before taking any action at all." Given these differences, collaboration should have been tense at best. But, an overriding strong corporate culture of openness and trust, coupled with strong team leadership that encouraged periodic social gatherings of team members and built a sense of "team," overcame these regional differences.

What is most important is to look beyond traditional organizational constructs, such as workgroups and geography, and look for areas of natural coalescence. Look for the existence of such groups in your organization, whether formed formally or informally. If you discover any, leverage them to their full potential for they possess the cultural fertile ground on which knowledge management can thrive.

BEYOND THE FOUR WALLS – SHARING KNOWLEDGE IN AN INTERCORPORATE ENVIRONMENT

They say that politics makes for strange bedfellows. Perhaps the same could soon be said of knowledge management. Coupled with the emerging powers of the Internet, organizations are beginning to create knowledge exchanges that transcend their four walls. Outsourcing and offshoring practices are creating fragmented, dispersed, yet highly functional organizations, comprised of many partners. On a more aggressive approach, vertical market exchanges, such as Covisint (overviewed in Chapter 5 along with the concept of global knowledge exchanges in which organizations sell their intellectual capital to would-be competitors) also require inter-corporate knowledge environments. Similarly, customers are being brought more tightly into the corporate knowledge base, participating in online collaboration in marketing and R&D. Knowledge chains and value chains are being extended to include all partners, customers, suppliers and, in some cases, competitors. The challenges facing business leaders today is to abandon current thought on how their businesses operate today and think more broadly and collaboratively (see Chapter 9 for resources that provide more insight on this issue).

TRUST AND LIABILITY – VULNERABILITY IN KNOWLEDGE SHARING

As we migrate to models that enable exchange of knowledge in an asynchronous manner, one in which the knowledge provider is unknown to the knowledge consumer, the issues of trust and liability become paramount.

Establishing credibility is a key roadblock to becoming a trusted knowledge exchange. Whether building on a corporate intranet, or a public Internet platform, the ability to provide trusted content – knowledge whose value and worth is "insured," so to speak – is of major concern. Even well-qualified sources may have a challenge in establishing credibility where no formal accreditation is available. In order to combat potential knowledge consumer apprehensions, approaches such as feedback mechanisms (e.g. consumers rate or vote on content value), screening processes (all input is subject to review before posting by a body of "authorities"), and linked résumés (overview of the knowledge provider is provided) have been designed as mechanisms to handle this issue.

Liability is more an issue in inter-organizational settings such as knowledge markets. Knowledge markets virtually always post a disclaimer regarding liability. As with anything else in the "real world," buyer beware.

OWNERSHIP OF KNOWLEDGE

A word of caution must be stated with regards to the approach to managing knowledge. If knowledge exists in the minds of those that use it, how can it be managed? "Management" infers control and external possession. In spite of what it may be called, the goal of knowledge management is to foster the sharing and leveraging of a collective knowledge base, not to take possession of it. Foster this idea in your community. Explain that knowledge will not be managed but cultivated. Demonstrate the reality of the approach you intend to "manage" knowledge. This can be done via the approaches taken to incentivization and leadership style. The task of knowledge leadership may, ultimately, not be so much to manage as it is to form agreement on the practices and methods by which the value of knowledge is interpreted.

ORGANIZATION – MAKING SENSE OF INFOGLUT

A fundamental challenge in building a knowledge base is in building a repository that can be effectively used by everyone in the organization. The party that is best equipped to organize or classify knowledge is the knowledge provider (he or she who has a clearer perspective and understanding of the knowledge, and can thus separate the wheat from the chaff). However, the knowledge provider frequently does not understand the precise knowledge requirements of the knowledge seeker, nor the specific context in which the knowledge seeker plans to apply the knowledge. The knowledge provider may also not know who the knowledge seeker is.

Conversely, the knowledge seeker understands the context in which the knowledge is to be applied, but does not understand the knowledge in sufficient depth or necessarily knows that it exists in order to search for it. To put it simply, the knowledge provider knows the answer, but not the question, and must thus organize the knowledge by attempting to second-guess the knowledge seeker's question.

Know that this is a real issue and meet it head on. Do not expect your users to "figure this one out." Much help is being supplied of late in the form of categorization tools. (This is one of the nine layers of functionality being addressed by portal vendors. See Chapter 4 for more details on categorization and portals.) These tools use a variety of linguistic, semantic, and statistical methods to automatically categorize content into like bodies of knowledge, building a corporate taxonomy that can be utilized as a navigational tool through the knowledge base and assist in knowledge discovery.

CONTENT MANAGEMENT, KNOWBOTS AND VIDEOGRAPHY

Also on the technology front, look to emerging functionality in content management, knowbots and videography.

Content management is partially related to the issue of trust discussed above. Software is being made available that will control and monitor the posting of information to Websites and portals, and provide means to keep it timely and ensure its authenticity.

On a more cutting edge, content management solutions provide the potential for one-to-one communication. By effectively integrating CRM and content management solutions, organizations have the ability to create a customized Web experience for their partners, prospects, and customers. The level of knowledge of these individuals is far greater than that of a random unidentified visitor, which provides for far greater levels of personalization. An organization, for example, can create personalized product catalogs for their top-tier clients that provide targeted product offerings, contracted prices, and direct billing capabilities.

Through the integration of business rules and data stored in ERP, BI, data warehouses, etc. (not viewable by the end user), content becomes a knowledge utilizer, leveraging the corporate knowledge base and guiding the user through the decision making process, asserting subtle, intelligent and targeted direction. Content is no longer simply brochure-ware, but an active participant in guiding the thought process. And while content management typically focuses on the delivery of text and graphic-based content, it must include in its arsenal virtually all information resources including databases (e.g. pricing lists), passwords, spreadsheets, etc.

Knowledge-based content management solutions also provide for proactive marketing. For example, an end user visits an e-commerce site and accesses information on several laptop computers, and then requests additional information about a specific model. The visitor's information is downloaded into the e-commerce firm's CRM system. Two weeks later, the product that the individual requested information about goes on sale. In response, the e-commerce site sends out a dynamically assembled e-mail to every visitor who requested information on that product. The company could do the same with new product releases, recalls, products updates, and myriad cross-selling opportunities.

Content management solutions can be used in proactive manners. Combining the personalization, search, and dynamic assembly functionality, high-end systems can integrate with agent and push technologies that will automatically send targeted relevant content to individuals based upon their user profile, or push particular products to viewers of an online catalog, based on current inventories and sales goals.

Knowbots are the latest generation of agent technology – knowledge-based search and discovery tools (i.e. internalization technology) that operate 24x7, in the background, keeping the knowledge seeker up to date, dynamically. Knowbots broker the information preferences of knowledge management system users through the multiple sources of content and processes accessible in the enterprise and on the business Web. The new role of content agency or content brokering, while it seems intuitively obvious, is in fact a bold shift in user experience on the Web or elsewhere. In a personalized model, the inherent promise is a shift away from a rigid machine interface, limiting what the user can see and how the system can be used, and toward a flexible interaction paradigm that allows the human to adjust parameters and content – in effect, allowing the human to design his or her own role- or job-based information environment and information "appliance."

Videography is a form of cognition and intermediation functionality (see Chapter 2 for more details on the basic applications of knowledge management). It is bleeding-edge technology that assists in the creation of implicit knowledge (see Chapter 2 for a definition of implicit knowledge). Some of the national laboratories are experimenting in this area. They are videotaping the daily routines of their top scientists, especially those nearing retirement. Their hope is that, by capturing the live action and interaction of these individuals, someday they will be able to create virtual agents that represent the expert, and pose new situations to them and see how they react. The eternal techno-optimist that I am, I see great value in this and am sure that one day it will be possible. But that day is probably decades away.

FREE AGENCY

Lastly, on the emerging trends from a business perspective, consider what the ability to broker knowledge over a linked global community can mean to the role of employee and experts. Based partially on the mechanics and models of the knowledge market, partially on the philosophy, culture and techniques of the extended enterprise and vortal, and grounded in now "traditional" business practices such as outsourcing, sub-contracting, consulting and temporary employment, knowledge workers may soon find themselves part of a growing group of freelance workers, not employed by any one "company," but utilized by many on an ad hoc basis, dynamically, as need and interest dictate. This evolving business model raises many issues and fuels some already addressed in this chapter. How do the contracting organizations ensure that the knowledge and experience gained by working with the free agent is externalized or assimilated into the corporate knowledge base? Indeed, do they own that knowledge? Non-disclosure and conflicts of interest will become a much more watched component of business dealings. The ability to create and maintain intermediation knowledge bases of resources outside the company will become a new measure of management success. (See Chapter 2 for a definition of intermediation and its role in knowledge management and Chapter 9 for resources that further the definition and debate over free agency.)

KEY LEARNING POINTS

» ROI – how to justify investments in knowledge management.
» Knowledge and leadership – is a CKO necessary?
» Culture – from corporate culture to regional cultures, how important are these issues and how should they be handled?
» Beyond the four walls – sharing knowledge in an intercorporate environment.

» Trust and liability – vulnerability in knowledge sharing.
» Ownership of knowledge.
» Organization – making sense of infoglut.
» Content management, knowbots and videography.
» Free agency.

07

Knowledge Management in Practice – Success Stories

What can we learn from those that have gone before? Knowledge management success stories include the following.

» Shell Oil – in deep water over knowledge management.
» Norske Skog Flooring – laying the ground to best sales practices.
» BAE Systems – changes in culture takes knowledge to new heights.

"If a little knowledge is dangerous, where is the man who has so much as to be out of danger?"

Thomas Henry Huxley

Knowledge management is applicable to virtually any organization, no matter the market, geographic location or age. However, the manifestation of knowledge management can be radically different, depending on the area of the business to which it is being applied, the product or end result required, and the culture of the organization. Here we look at an array of companies, from around the globe, in various markets. Each has been successful with implementing a knowledge management practice. Yet, as you will see, each has a very different story to tell: different challenges, different cultures to overcome, different customers and different approaches to solution design and justification. What they all have in common is a clear sense of purpose, a strategy, a known audience and insight into the needs of the population (for more detail on why these issues are prerequisites to a knowledge management initiative, see Chapter 10).

SHELL OIL – IN DEEP WATER OVER KNOWLEDGE MANAGEMENT

In the early 1990s, Shell, like all oil companies around the globe, was faced with a new opportunity. But, like so many new opportunities, this one was coupled with new challenges. The opportunity existed in the potential to increase oil production by tapping into oil fields discovered in deep water. The challenge lay in the fact that oil production was never before executed in the environment of the deep ocean. Existing production and exploration approaches and technologies would not work, that much was clear. But the potential revenue and competitive advantage was great enough to seriously investigate how safe and profitable oil extraction form the ocean floor might be accomplished. Recognizing the complexity of the issue, and the time pressures due to competition, Shell decided that it had to do more than just re-examine its use of technology. It recognized that in order to expedite this effort it would need to step up its ability to learn and innovate. Business practices and communication styles were equally scrutinized.

At the start of the project, Shell's Deep Water Division was constructed like all other teams within Shell. The division consisted of two units, exploration and production. Each unit was comprised of departments aligned against functional specialties. The exploration teams were responsible for determining the potential value of a field. The production teams were responsible for developing the project. Given the size and immaturity of deep-water exploration, it was critical for both units to be in constant communication. But, as is often the case with functional groups, cross-communication was burdened with formal protocols. Communication between exploration and production, as well as among their individual teams, was difficult, slow and complex. For example, maps created by exploration were often redrawn and tweaked by production to meet their needs.

In an effort to change knowledge culture, facilitate communication and thus hopefully increase the rate of innovation, Shell decided to reorganize the deep-water team into three main divisions. As part of this effort, cross-functional teams became a main organizational structure within each division. The divisions were formed around geographical areas, called assets. These asset teams were comprised of people from all disciplines – from scientist to engineer. All members of the asset team reported to a single project manager. Staffing levels and composition were altered as the project progressed, adding and deleting specific talents as necessary. But the core asset team remained as an entity. Each asset team was given great autonomy. Each operated its own profit and loss, responsible for the entire life cycle of the project from scientific analysis to financial return.

This change in team composition and reporting structure immediately changed the way people worked and communicated. As members of an asset team, individuals were more aware of how the work of one impacted the other. More importantly, different perspectives were more easily provided. Creative thought flowed more easily among different disciplines. For example, comments made by a geologist could be contemplated by a reservoir engineer. This change in structure created a new group and individual dynamic that allowed staff to focus on a big goal and exercise a give-and-take attitude versus a "my goal" and "I do what I need to do to get my job done" attitude.

To support the efforts of the individual teams, Shell also created a centralized group that represented its core competencies. This centralized department housed the best of the best thinkers in specific vertical areas of expertise. These ''experts'' made themselves available to the teams and acted as liaison between the asset teams and the company research lab.

But this solution created a problem – as solutions often do. Unforeseen at the time, the cross-functional teams made it more difficult for functional groups to communicate. The knowledge shared among similar specialists was waning. For example, geophysicists openly communicated and collaborated with the members of their asset teams, but were no longer collaborated with and learned from other geophysicists. Functional silos had been replaced with team silos. Recognizing this, Shell put in place a team to assess the new challenges. This team discovered that:

There was no standard process in place for sharing knowledge between teams. Cross-team knowledge transfer was potentially very valuable, but a lack of formalized and standard approaches to facilitate this type of collaboration hindered it from occurring.

Functional knowledge sharing became slower and, as a result, learning and adapting was delayed within each functional group.

Though team members knew the value of sharing lessons learned, there was no time with which to do this. Documentation was considered a luxury afforded to few. From management to worker, focus was on production. Subliminally, messages were sent that knowledge sharing could not interfere with team progress. Furthermore, there were no standard approaches or infrastructure for disseminating lessons learned. Asset team members, willing to share knowledge, were unsure as to the level of detail that needed to be captured and shared. The documentation that did exist was fragmented, in many locations and different formats. This led to an information management problem. The documentation that did exist was too difficult to locate. The change management team calculated that approximately 40 percent of an individual's time was spent looking for existing information.

Based on these observations, the change management team instituted the following changes as part of the knowledge management initiative.

Learning communities were established. These communities were built around topics important to business and community members. They were functional teams comprised of individuals – from across many asset teams – that shared a similar technical role. Recognizing that teams needed some structure in order to facilitate knowledge communication, the teams were given regularly staged forums in which to meet. But, also recognizing that the specific knowledge needs of each team would be different, each community was given the autonomy to create their own standards for capturing and sharing knowledge. The teams were given access to Web-based technology to augment this process.

Additionally, a knowledge community infrastructure team (KNIT) was formed to provide guidance and support of the knowledge management effort on each learning community and asset team. This team also provided Web development services to the asset teams and learning communities, and access to other tools for knowledge capture and dissemination. Each Website and family of tools was designed for the specific needs of each team. This was not a one-size-fits-all solution. But, in each instance, the knowledge repositories were originally housed in a push environment. Under this environment, the owners/writers of the lessons learned determined what value was contained in the lesson. It was pushed out to others, all at once. Shell discovered that this was ineffective. Often users would receive knowledge that was not timely, not yet relevant. This was typically forgotten. Augmenting the system with sophisticated pull, or internalization technology (see Chapter 3 for more details on internalization technology), allowed users to intuitively extract knowledge in a just in time manner. More importantly, the knowledge was discovered based on the consumer's needs and perspectives, not those of the knowledge provider.

Each community had its own leader. The role of this individual was more in human and group dynamic management and promotion. The leaders were not active members of their respective communities per se. They acted more as knowledge stewards (see Chapter 8 for more details on the role of a knowledge steward). To ensure ongoing quality of the communities and teams, a peer review process was put in place.

This also gave the opportunity to monitor and track the quality of individual knowledge input.

Shell noted that, despite the fact that each community was provided autonomy on how to specifically operate, a best practice did emerge that serves today as a blueprint. This included the consistent holding of weekly meetings that were agenda-less (i.e. open for free discussion), hosting presentations by vendors of technology to augment the capture and sharing of explicit knowledge, establishing a common data library, and establishing a community coordinator focused on team dynamics.

It is interesting to note that, while Shell knew that establishing these knowledge communities was an important step to be taken, they also realized that they could not anticipate all the needs of each team. They rolled these communities out on a "learn and adapt as we go" basis – one team at a time, and the lessons learned were used to redo how the next team would roll out. Constant revaluation. By 1998 the team formation was going well. The learning team then focused on cross-team communication. Only loose rules and procedures were originally provided on how teams should cross-coordinate. It is also important to note that, as the formalization of recognition for knowledge sharing emerged, it became institutionalized, or made official, so to speak, by incorporating such review into official employee performance appraisals. By 1999 there were 16 active learning communities within the Deep Water Division of Shell.

Where did all of this lead? The KNIT group defined two basic benefits that were realized: reduced costs and improved accuracy and quality. Several specific occurrences were pointed to as examples of reduction in cost. By sharing what was known, best practices got replicated and saved the company money. Examples included the ability to develop a site using three wells instead of four, which saved the company $2–3 million. Increased awareness of safety best practices resulted in a 1 percent increase in uptime. If this sounds insignificant, think again: at Shell, this amounted to $150,000/day savings. Centralized best practices in procuring chemicals resulted in a cost reduction of over 60 percent in this area.

Improved accuracy and quality manifested in several ways as well. Identifiable circumvention of errors not only improved quality but also saved money. For example, by identifying an erroneous approach to storing data to a map site, one site avoided $1-2 million in mistakes. If this was not caught until after the well was drilled then it could have amounted to a much greater cost – in the tens of millions.

KEY KNOWLEDGE MANAGEMENT INSIGHTS AT SHELL

Shell used a simple and popular approach to facilitating knowledge transfer: multi-disciplinary teams. This approach to organizational structure has often proven most valuable in providing cross-functional collaboration.

They also discovered, however, that knowledge management is a practice that requires constant vigilance and redefinition. Creation of the asset teams created the unforeseen issue of decreased functional-level communication. Shell responded properly by instituting the KNIT group.

This is also a classic example of a successful knowledge management system that involved cultural and structural changes far more than technology changes, which were introduced some considerable time later. Technology was properly viewed and instituted as an augmenter to the knowledge management practice, not the practice itself.

As part of the cultural change, to a more knowledge-sharing environment, Shell understood the value of providing autonomy and a spirit of entrepreneurship. Teams were set up as their own profit and loss centers. This strengthens a sense of belonging. While basic rules were provided, teams and communities were empowered to determine their fate, the approaches required, the level of knowledge needed, etc. Not only does this also foster a sense of team and camaraderie, it also recognizes that knowledge is a personal thing. Typically, a one-size-fits-all approach across an organization will not suffice.

But, flying almost in the face of this is the fact that teams/people do need and want some rules. As Shell discovered after its early attempts at knowledge-based teams, without any boundaries and definitions people flounder. Knowledge may be personal but, to bring any order to it, guidelines must be provided as to the level of detail that should be captured, when it should be captured and how to value it. Similarly, Shell discovered that knowledge management requires leadership. In their case, that leadership took the form of a change management team and individual knowledge stewards.

Shell also learned that while technology was not their answer, it was a most valuable enabler, if used correctly. Providing internalization technology to team members allowed for just in time extraction of knowledge. This technology also provided input to an ROI scenario, greatly decreasing the time spent looking for knowledge. This is an often-encountered situation.

The importance of providing time for sharing and formal recognition of knowledge sharing was learned by Shell. Too often management may speak of knowledge sharing but, if no time is provided in which to do it, it will not be done. If official corporate policy, reviews, job descriptions and the like are not in place that specifically encourage and reward knowledge sharing, it will not happen.

But perhaps the biggest lesson learned from this vast study is the fact that knowledge management is an agent of change. It will bring change to the organization in unanticipated ways. Knowledge requires an ongoing commitment to its management, with changes made along the way to handle the unforeseen issues that will arise. Shell's knowledge management solution did not occur in one major step, but in the execution of several steps, spaced out by efforts of investigation and evaluation.

NORSKE SKOG FLOORING – LAYING THE GROUND TO BEST SALES PRACTICES

Norske Skog Flooring (NSF) is one of Europe's largest manufacturers of flooring materials. When R&D developed Alloc, an interlocking flooring system, NSF realized that it had not developed a new product, but a whole new category in flooring materials. This posed a new challenge to NSF. They needed to go beyond a simple marketing roll out. They needed an effective and cost-efficient means to get the rest of the flooring industry to see the merits of the new product category. Without proper appreciation for the new product line, however, it was clear that the buying community would not see the value and the return on the product would be minimized. Clearly, product launch would require more than traditional training methods and brochureware. Salespeople posed a particularly large issue, as salespeople do not consistently have a deep knowledge of their products. Knowledge ranged from that of a craftsperson to a salesperson in the truest sense of that word, with no first-hand knowledge of products or industry.

The answer to this knowledge problem came by way of a popular knowledge management practice: collaboration. NSF collaborated with Scandinavian Celemi's Launch and Branding Division, which specialized in creating learning tools and processes to support marketing efforts. Together, they decided to create a marketing program that would allow NSF personnel to easily demonstrate the features and benefits of this flooring system to distributors, retailers, installers, etc. in a personalized and interactive manner. The solution was based in a marketing specialty from Celemi known as Learning Marketing. The approach did not force information on to sales professionals; rather, the approach allowed sales personnel to discover what they needed to learn, and then facilitate that learning process in a just in time fashion. Knowledge would be delivered in customized sessions, tailored to different learning levels and backgrounds. The learning processes would be entertaining and interactive. And, most of all, it would be easy.

NSF's knowledge management-based marketing did make specific use of technology. Unencumbered by the constraints of paper-based marketing approaches, the Learning Marketing system amply used online simulations and teamwork-based interactions. By "walking the student" through the entire flooring life cycle, installers, retailers, retail sales and distributors were exposed to the total value of Alloc, and thus were able to talk about value-add, not just pricing.

The learning process deployed by Learning Marketing uses a six-step learning process: create an interest; supply just enough information – just in time; provide exercises to allow the processing of knowledge; provide points of conclusion to reinforce sense of achievement;

let users experience how their insights can be applied to real word scenarios; provide ongoing and continuous follow-up.

At the core of this knowledge management system were four WorkMarts, interactive visually oriented screens, customized to reflect the current issues and concerns of flooring personnel, i.e. installers, distributors and retailers. The WorkMarts incorporated the experience and knowledge (both tacit and explicit) of industry experts in their respective fields into the training and sample scenarios. Real-life examples/experiences, industry statistics and best practices were incorporated into each WorkMart.

In the first WorkMart, sales professionals work in a team to analyze the nature of "their" store. Using WorkMart they collaborate on issues such as currently available flooring options, the merits and trade-offs of each, and buying habits and reasoning processes seen in customers. They are provided the opportunity to open their own simulated store and interact with simulated customers. Several customer profiles are available from which to choose, such as "Price is not an issue as long as I get what I want," and "I want it now."

In the second WorkMart, students interact with the Alloc product. Students can match design features to corresponding benefits. This was designed to reinforce the lessons learned, and provide immediate gratification through success.

The third WorkMart introduces new customers with specific questions about the product to the student. Using role-playing techniques, the students can prepare different answers, and determine the eventual results. This serves to sharpen product knowledge and the interactive skills of the student.

In the fourth WorkMart, the students participate in project installations, develop price quotes for various jobs, and work hands-on with the product to get a sense for the ease of installation.

Participants in the learning process ranked the training very highly. Consistently they ranked three features that made the learning exercise effective: the novel approach of the training was engaging, it was simple, and it fostered teamwork and knowledge-sharing opportunities that increased effectiveness and retention.

Those who complete the course are presented with a certificate of completion. Participating retailers are tracked and supplied with updates to the training. Feedback is solicited and incorporated into WorkMart updates. Store performance is measured. Results are passed along to distributors to encourage continued interest.

As for results, stores that underwent the Alloc Learning Program training had sales 50 percent higher than those that did not. The program's success is perhaps best illustrated by the fact that NSF did not have to offer traditional additional incentives, such as bonuses, to encourage sales of their product.

KEY KNOWLEDGE MANAGEMENT INSIGHTS AT NORSKE SKOG FLOORING

Several issues associated with this case study are particularly interesting. First, it is interesting to note that this case study highlights the importance of collaboration. Not only did NSF meet their knowledge challenge by collaborating with expertise from an outside party, Celemi, but also within the solution, collaboration was encouraged at various points of the learning exercise. As was seen in the Shell case study (see above), cross-team collaboration brings specific benefit. By involving all participants with the full life cycle of a flooring product, each was better prepared to best represent the product and answer virtually any type of question. Participants specifically identified the collaboration as a major reason for the program's success and appeal.

Second, the case illustrates a particular type of deployment or application of knowledge management: e-learning. E-learning seeks to incorporate tacit and explicit knowledge into online instruction that is typically interactive and customized to meet the needs of individuals, rather than groups. Clearly, this was the case in the NSF Learning Marketing application. As an e-learning application, this knowledge management solution did focus heavily on technology, almost from the outset. The flexibility of online knowledge transfer enabled NSF to provide training in a manner simply impossible in a paper-based approach.

Third, the value of implicit knowledge (the capturing of expertise from leaders in their respective fields and incorporating this into the WorkMarts) is also a highlight of this case study. It was this approach that made the WorkMarts believable and valuable from a practical perspective (see Chapter 2 for more detail on implicit knowledge).

Lastly, NSF also demonstrated the value of incentivization and recognition in knowledge management. The incorporation of immediate feedback during the training sessions provided gratification in the form of success. The simple act of providing certificates of completion and ongoing performance rankings to participants also had a positive effect, encouraging initial cooperation and ongoing interest.

BAE SYSTEMS – CHANGES IN CULTURE TAKES KNOWLEDGE TO NEW HEIGHTS

BAE Systems (BAE), formerly British Aerospace, is a leading manufacturer of aerospace and defense systems. Headquartered in the UK, it has home offices in the USA, Canada, Germany, Italy, Australia, Saudi Arabia, and Sweden. In the early 1990s, BAE saw its market radically change. Globally, governments were slashing defense budgets. Mergers and acquisitions, particularly in the USA, caused changes in supply-side economics.

In 1998, in order to address these market changes, BAE decided to make some cultural changes. At the time, their culture was characterized as separate fiefdoms in the commercial and defense sectors of the company.

The knowledge management initiative was started by assembling 130 business unit managers in a forum called Benchmark BAe. Managers were asked to identify and share existing goals and conditions that would contribute to the creation of a more collaborative organization, steeped in knowledge sharing. The forum resulted in the capture of the following observations: people represent BAE's greatest strength; customers are the number one priority; the future of the company lies in partnering; innovation and technology provide a competitive edge; and performance must be measured to ensure success.

While realization of this list was a noble and valuable task, the exercise also vicariously started to stir the pot. Managers began thinking outside their own domains and in non-traditional ways to define success and value. (For some participants, this was the first time they had ever met, let alone shared, ideas.)

This group later discussed findings with a wider group that included virtually all mid-level management. These focus groups built on top of the value statements and identified specific practices, behaviors and methods that supported and nurtured the value statements. This resulted in the formation of five teams, each tasked with addressing one of the five value statements. Their goal was to develop a corporate-wide list of values that would be disseminated throughout the business units. This plan, known as the "value plan," continues to thrive as an evergreen project, making modifications based on vigilant monitoring.

The initial and ongoing success of these five teams was founded in the fact that BAE developed an evaluation tool, based upon the predefined corporate values, which verifies that the patterns of behavior exhibited by the unit managers are aligned with the five value statements. This tool is an intranet application that provides self-evaluation. The results of the evaluation are provided to the respective manager, the CEO and the project manager. Eventually BAE plans on a 360° evaluation for all employees. Additionally, over 1500 line managers have available to them a training program that: seeks to establish a common appreciation and understanding of the business, the respective team, and the role of line manager; teaches the application of efficient managerial techniques in order to manage change; provides 360° feedback from peers and staff before and after the training; builds awareness of the necessary abilities to coach and support team value planning; and teaches the techniques and tools necessary to demonstrate leadership by example. This program, known as BEST, is planned for incorporation into management development programs.

In parallel, BAE created the virtual university (VU) in 1997. With VU, the company instituted a collaborative forum that partners with academic and business thought leaders in the area of knowledge management. Jointly, VU staff develops best practices and content. Experienced business unit managers act as the deans and directors of the university and VU acts as a corporate center for lifelong learning, research and development, best practices and an open knowledge exchange. Within VU, internal and external best practices are organized and brokered to requesting knowledge seekers. The knowledge captured is both explicit (e.g. a written best practice or proven approach to a particular process) and tacit (e.g. tracking and identification of experts in particular areas).

But, as progress was made in acquiring knowledge, the issue of infoglut began to make its mark on BAE and the VU. For example, by the end of 1999, the best practices database had over 300 entries. On April 13, 2000 the VU held one of its regularly scheduled learning days. In addition to 140 participants that attended in person, 1400 participants attended through the worldwide virtual forum.

Situations such as these caused BAE to examine its then current search and knowledge sharing habits. BAE Systems discovered that over 80 percent of employees were spending an average of 30 minutes a day retrieving information, while 60 percent were spending an hour or more duplicating the work of others. By front-ending the knowledge management systems, including the VU, with intermediation and internalization toolsets (see Chapter 3 for more details on knowledge management technology) the ease with which knowledge sources are found was increased and speed of location was dramatically decreased. This functionality not only allows users to search for knowledge, but will push or alert BAE employees to documents in the system that relate to what they're doing, or to other employees in the company whose interests and expertise match their own.

Although a formal ROI has not been conducted, BAE managers feel they have met their objectives. As one BAE manger put it, ''We discovered engineers working, in different parts of the country, on precisely the same problem – a wing construction issue – but in very different areas, a military aircraft and an airbus. One group took the step to establish best practice, which was transferred to another plant in another geographical location with multi-million pound savings.'' Although the knowledge management practice cannot be attributed directly to all of its success, BAE went from being the fourth largest aerospace company in the world in 1997 to, currently, the second largest. Today, BAE is a more competitive player in the aerospace industry. By changing corporate culture, its employees do not function as a group of separate sectors, but as one organization, tasked with a central mission.

Note: in 1999, VU won the US Corporate University Xchange Excellence Award, co-sponsored by *The Financial Times*, for its innovative utilization of technology to create a continuous learning environment for all BAE employees.

KEY KNOWLEDGE MANAGEMENT INSIGHTS AT BAE

One important reason this initiative succeeded was BAE's initial effort to get virtually everyone involved. All unit managers and, subsequently mid-level managers participated in the knowledge management definition process.

Similarly, BAE started the design process with the development of a mission statement and a succinct, well-articulated set of core competencies, what they called the five value statements. Subsequent efforts were consistently aligned along these statements. This is a best practice in developing a knowledge management practice. Everyone in the organization needs to be made clearly aware of what the bottom line goals of the initiative are. This provides the beacon to which they can all look (see Chapter 10, step 2 for more details on the role of critical success factors in a knowledge management initiative).

BAE also demonstrates the value of keeping a knowledge management practice evergreen. Mechanisms have been put in place so staff can continuously measure how well they continue to align along the value statements. Furthermore, measures and benchmarks were put in place to allow for consistent measurement of progress (see Chapter 10, steps 9 and 10, for more detail on the importance of benchmarks and cyclical analysis).

From a technology standpoint, the BAE case study highlights the often-found value in powerful internalization functionality and knowbots, in facilitating the dynamic discovery of both explicit and tacit knowledge from an otherwise undifferentiated mass. (See Chapter 4 for more detail on internalization technology and Chapter 6 for more detail on knowbots.)

08

Key Concepts and Thinkers in Knowledge Management

A look at the language of knowledge, including:

» a glossary of terms used in the knowledge management lexicon; and
» overviews of key thinkers in the world of knowledge management.

"The greatest difficulty lies not in persuading people to accept new ideas, but in persuading them to abandon old ones."
John Maynard Keynes, twentieth-century economist

THE LANGUAGE OF KNOWLEDGE: A GLOSSARY OF TERMS

Agents (agent technology) – Software programs that transparently execute 24×7 procedures to support gathering, delivering, categorizing, profiling information or notifying the knowledge seeker about the existence of, or changes, in an area of interest.

Asynchronous communication – The ability of two or more individuals to accomplish work from different places/different time modes by using a process intermediary. Knowledge management tools can perform the work of bridging time and space. In the asynchronous communication model, the process has intelligence to understand the rules and monitoring parameters that must be captured and conveyed to process participants.

Categorization – One of the nine functional elements of a portal, and the genre of software tools that support this functionality. Categorization creates a taxonomy of the knowledge base and tracks knowledge objects in this taxonomy. The resulting model can aid in navigating the knowledge body. A form of Externalization.

CKO (Chief Knowledge Officer) – See Knowledge leadership.

Cognition – The ability to synthesize diverse sources of information in making a decision. The aspect of knowledge management solutions used to facilitate decision making.

Community of practice – Communities that form within an organization where people assume roles based on their abilities and skills instead of titles and hierarchical stature. Also referred to as community of interest.

Competency management – The ability to use knowledge management to consistently facilitate the formation of new ideas, products, and services that support the core competency of the organization.

Concept-based search – A form of content-based indexing, search and retrieval in which the search engine possesses a level of intelligence regarding semantics and lexicons. In such a system, internalization and externalization can be achieved at a conceptual level, providing results far beyond that of word-based queries.

Concept-to-cash – The time required to bring a new idea from inception/conception to market. See Knowledge chain.

Content management – A form of knowledge management software and practices that tracks and controls the accuracy of content in the knowledge body, and links the content to business rules, applications and other bodies of content to provide customized, intelligent usage of the content in an automated and dynamic fashion.

Content mapping – The process of identifying and organizing a high-level description of the meaning contained in a collection of electronic documents. Content maps are usually rendered as hierarchical "outlines," but many kinds of more suggestive displays are available through graphical visualization techniques. Content maps are used to facilitate the comprehension of the knowledge base. A form of portal categorization functionality.

Context sensitivity – The ability of a knowledge management system to provide insight that takes into consideration the contextual nature of a user's request based on history, associations, and subject matter experience.

Contribution monitoring and valuation – A method for analyzing the relative value of an individual's knowledge-supporting activities in a knowledge management system, utilizing a variety of metrics, which could include the following electronically-based approaches:

» numbers of contributions to knowledge forums;
» numbers of successful problem resolutions associated with an individual's contributions;
» amount of message traffic targeted to take advantage of an individual's expertise, etc.

Core competency – The overriding value statement of an organization. Core competency differs from product and market competency in that an organization's core competency outlives product life cycles and market swings.

Core rigidity – Opposite of core competency. Defining any core competency too narrowly may turn it into a core rigidity. Core rigidities are unquestioned assumptions about an organization's products, policies, or positioning that lead to complacency and inhibit new innovation.

Customer capital – Customer capital refers to the value, usually not reflected in accounting systems other than as goodwill, which results from the relationships an organization has built with its customers. One of three forms of intellectual capital as defined by Edvinsson and Stewart. Customer capital is a component of external awareness and represents the value of the bond between you and your customers. This is not just a matter of brand loyalty. Customer capital considers how well you are able to understand your customers, their changing needs and requirements. Its value is at least equal to the cost of creating a new customer. See Structural capital and Human capital.

Dilemma of incentivization – A paradox that arises out of the structural imbalance between knowledge seekers and knowledge providers. The knowledge provider, while able to provide knowledge, typically has little or no incentive to do so. The knowledge seeker is highly incentivized to receive the knowledge, but is unable to do so without the cooperation of the knowledge provider. See Dilemma of organization.

Dilemma of organization (structure) – A phenomenon or paradox that arises out of the asymmetry between knowledge seekers and knowledge providers relative to knowledge content. The knowledge provider is well equipped to provide structure to the knowledge, but typically does not know the context in which it might be used later. The knowledge seeker is intimately familiar with the context of the required knowledge, but does not understand the knowledge in sufficient depth to organize it or appreciate its structure. See Dilemma of incentivization.

Disintermediation – The elimination of middle layers of management control and other internal or external intermediaries. The benefit is a faster execution of the knowledge chain.

Discontinuity of knowledge – A phenomenon that occurs when experienced knowledge workers move from one position to another position (inside or outside an organization) without having adequate time or knowledge management facilities to transfer their tacit knowledge to co-workers.

Document management – A software system based on an underlying database, in which unstructured objects (i.e. documents) are indexed and tracked. Document management systems monitor security, log access to files, and maintain a history of file content. Within a knowledge management system, document management can provide an automated approach to externalization and internalization. In more advanced systems, user profiles can be maintained as an object. In these cases, the owners of tacit knowledge are tracked and made available as a known resource through user queries via Electronic Yellow Pages.

Electronic Yellow Pages – An online listing of personnel, their competencies and their contact information. Within a knowledge management environment, the Yellow Pages are prefaced with a profile of each user's experiences and areas of expertise. Queries on the profiles will result in a list of known individuals that should possess expert tacit knowledge on the query's subject matter. In a heuristic electronic Yellow Pages the system can infer competencies by observing an individual's behaviors and work product.

Explicit knowledge – One of the two types of knowledge, whose taxonomy was most notably espoused by Michael Polanyi. Explicit knowledge is knowledge that is easily codified and conveyed to others. See Tacit knowledge.

External awareness – A component of the knowledge chain, which represents an organization's ability to understand the market's perceived value of its products and services as well as the changing directions and requirements of its markets. When coupled with internal awareness, external awareness can lead to the discovery of successful new markets. See Knowledge chain.

Externalization – The transfer of knowledge from the minds of its holders to an external repository in the most efficient way possible. Externalization tools help build knowledge maps. They capture and organize incoming bodies of explicit knowledge and create clusters of bodies of knowledge.

External responsiveness – A component of the knowledge chain that emphasizes the ability to meet the market on its own terms even when the market cannot articulate these. It is a level of responsiveness to environmental conditions that is significantly faster and based on better connections between resources and markets. See Knowledge chain.

Federated Search – A form of externalization functionality. Federated search makes discovery of explicit content simpler by propagating a single user request for knowledge across multiple repositories (e.g. e-mail systems, document management systems and web sites.) and consolidating the knowledge resources into a single list.

Federation – A form of organizational structure where the value chain is loosely organized as an alliance of independent but reliant organizations or work cells in lieu of departments or divisions within a single enterprise.

Free agency – The lowest level of granularity in a free market workforce. Free agents are effectively organizations of one, which come together temporarily to form project-based alliances.

Heuristic software – A software solution that learns about its users and the knowledge they possess by monitoring the user's interaction with the system. Thus, over time, its ability to provide users with relevant knowledge should improve. A form of the portal learning loop. See Learning loop and Suggestive software.

Human capital – The collective value of an organization's know-how. Human capital refers to the value, usually not reflected in accounting systems, which results from the investment an organization must make to recreate the knowledge in its employees. One of three forms of intellectual capital as defined by Edvinsson and Stewart. A component of internal awareness. See Structural capital and Customer capital.

Implicit knowledge – A form of knowledge derived from the careful and deliberate decomposing of certain bodies of tacit knowledge into a series of quantifiable and codifiable series of explicit knowledge. See also Explicit knowledge and Tacit knowledge.

Increasing returns (Theory of) – Economic theory created by a group of economists (prominently, Brian Arthur and Paul Romer) which proposes that the emerging information economy, with its shift of value from raw materials and manufactured goods to information itself, requires a new economic model based on the dynamic of increasing returns of scale. The primary example is the software market, where successful producers have increasing returns to scale (each new unit of output returns incrementally more profit than the last) because of variable costs approaching zero in volume production, as well as "network externalities," and "lock-in." In contrast, in the classical economy, businesses faced inevitably decreasing returns to scale as increasingly larger plants eventually reached a point where marginal increases in production required marginal increases in cost.

Information Architecture – a component to externalization and internalization. Information architecture involves the design, organization, and navigation of information systems specifically to facilitate user discovery and interaction with explicit knowledge.

Intellectual capital – Intellectual capital can be segmented into three sub-categories: human capital, structural capital, and customer capital. Although acknowledged as valuable in most organizations, these assets are not measured and accounted for in most organizations' financial statements other than as goodwill. Many believe these assets form the basis for most equity market valuations of an organization. Intellectual capital represents the sum total of what your employees know. Its value is at least equal to the cost of recreating this knowledge.

Intermediation – The brokerage function that brings together knowledge seekers (questions) with knowledge providers (answers). Intermediation technologies facilitate the connections between people and the communication of knowledge between seeker and provider. One of four key knowledge management functions. See Knowledge mapping, Externalization, Internalization, and Cognition.

Internal awareness – A component of the knowledge chain that represents an organization's collective understanding of its strengths and weaknesses across structural silos and functional boundaries. Internal awareness is not only having your house in order, but also knowing what order your house is in. See Knowledge chain.

Internalization – The transfer of explicit knowledge from an external repository (temporary or permanent) to an individual, in the most useful and efficient way possible. There are two aspects to internalization: extraction and filtering. One of four key knowledge management functions. See Knowledge mapping, Externalization, Internalization, and Cognition.

Internal responsiveness – A component of the knowledge chain that represents an organization's ability to instantly organize skills based on an unfiltered assessment of its resources and external market demands and opportunities. See Knowledge chain.

Knowledge architect – See Knowledge leadership.

Knowledge audit – An assessment of an organization's propensity for knowledge management, current achievements in knowledge management, its current knowledge ecology, and the mapping of available tacit and explicit knowledge resources. Knowledge audits provide critical and objective insight into the targeted organization's formal and informal knowledge practices, influences on these, best practices and worst practices. Audits identify what an organization should do to maximize its payback from knowledge management.

Knowledge base – Typically used to describe any collection of information that also includes contextual or experiential references to other metadata.

Knowledge broker – A person, organization, or process that identifies intersections between knowledge seekers (buyers) and knowledge providers (sellers) and creates a vehicle for linking the two.

Knowledge chain – The flow of knowledge through four definitive stages in this chain: internal awareness, internal responsiveness, external awareness, and external responsiveness.

Knowledge concierge – A title adopted by some organizations for individuals who have the responsibility of facilitating the transfer of knowledge across communities of practice. See Knowledge broker.

Knowledge ecology – The component of knowledge management that focuses on human factors, namely, the study of personal work habits, values, and organizational culture.

Knowledge engineer – See Knowledge leadership.

Knowledge guild – A descriptive term for an organized group of suppliers of a specific kind of knowledge. Knowledge guilds guarantee a level of quality in business interactions with their members. This guarantee differentiates guild members from others who might be active in "selling" similar knowledge in a knowledge bazaar.

Knowledge half-life – The point at which the acquisition of new knowledge is more cost-effective and offers greater returns than the maintenance of existing knowledge.

Knowledge leadership (Types of) – Knowledge leadership represents a broad category of positions and responsibilities, from individuals who literally fall into the de facto position of knowledge manager, with no change in title, formal responsibilities or compensation, to very well-compensated senior executives who are recruited specifically for the role of CKO. Although no taxonomy could possibly set forth all the titles and responsibilities included under knowledge leadership, the following typify the general categories you are likely to encounter today:

» **Chief Knowledge Officer** – responsible for enterprise-wide coordination of all knowledge leadership. The CKO typically is chartered by the CEO and is often (but not always) part of IT. The CKO's focus is the practice of knowledge leadership and the role is usually that of a solo performer with no immediate LOB responsibility. Before a culture of knowledge sharing, incentives, and the basic precepts of knowledge leadership have been acknowledged by the enterprise, the CKO is powerless.

» **Knowledge analyst** – collects, organizes, and disseminates knowledge, usually on demand. They provide knowledge leadership by becoming walking repositories of best practices, a library of how knowledge is and needs to be shared across an organization. There is a risk that these individuals become so valuable to their immediate constituency that they are not able to move laterally to other parts of the organization where their skills are equally needed.

» **Knowledge engineer** – converts explicit knowledge to instructions and programs systems and codified applications. Effectively, the better knowledge engineers codify knowledge, the harder it is for the organization to change when their environment demands it.

» **Knowledge manager** – coordinates the efforts of engineers, architects, and analysts. The knowledge manager is most often required in large organizations where the numbers of discrete knowledge-sharing processes risk fragmentation and isolation. The risk in having knowledge managers is that fiefdoms (albeit large ones) may begin to form around the success of each manager's domain.

» **Knowledge steward** – provides minimal, ongoing support to knowledge users in the form of expertise in the tools, practices and methods of knowledge leadership. The steward is usually an individual who has fallen into the role of helping others better understand and leverage the power of new technologies and practices in managing knowledge.

Knowledge management – The leveraging of collective wisdom to increase responsiveness and innovation.

Knowledge manager – See Knowledge leadership.

Knowledge mapping (knowledge taxonomy) – A process that provides a picture of the specific knowledge it requires in order to support its business processes.

Knowledge market (knowledge bazaar, info souk, etc.) – An online gathering place where owners of intellectual property can barter, sell and otherwise exchange their intellectual property for value. Such markets may be undifferentiated, e.g. knowledge bazaars; organized through knowledge brokers; or modulated through the instrument of the knowledge guild.

Knowledge providers/seller – An individual that possesses knowledge of value to other individuals.

Knowledge seeker/buyer – An individual that needs to access knowledge held by another individual or stored in a repository.

Knowledge steward – See Knowledge leadership.

Knowledge topology – A framework that segments knowledge management into four key categories: intermediation, externalization, internalization, and cognition.

Learning loop – One of the nine layers of functionality in a portal. Heuristic software that monitors and tracks access trends and knowledge requirements for each user, and automatically makes changes to the portal based on these observations. See also Portal.

Learning organization – An organization with the necessary practices, culture, and systems to promote the continuous sharing of experience and lessons learned. Popularized by Senge. Knowledge management systems seek to identify through knowledge mapping, and to implement through competency management, the kinds of specific organizational and individual learning that must take place if the business is to build and maintain the required competencies to compete effectively.

Linguistic analysis – A form of concept-based retrieval in which semantic networks, lexicons and parsers are used to determine the overall subject matter of a body of text.

Matrix organization – The synthesis of central control and decentralization structures within a single organization. A matrix organization is typically organized around task forces or teams consisting of functional members.

Metadata – Data that provides context or otherwise describes information in order to make it more valuable as part of a knowledge management system. Metadata is most often used to connect information in relevant ways to people, process, or product.

Metaskills – The basic tool of generative learning. These skills are aimed at ensuring three things: skills adaptability, autonomous decision making, and an emotional aptitude for change.

Ontology – A form of internalization, used to intelligent link knowledge sources/resources by declared relationship types. Can be used to create knowledge maps. A network of relationship types used to track how sources of knowledge relate to one another. For example, a "lives at" link or "works for" link in an ontology would be used to track these relationships for listed individuals. Similar to a thesaurus, but supports the definition of contextual, customizable, self describing relationships. Ontology is the framework of the semantic web, and permits intelligent navigation.

Organized abandonment – The process by which new innovations replace current products before the current product is out of its profit zone. See Profit zone.

Portal – A user-customizable single point of access (SPOA) to the knowledge objects and related processes in a defined community.

Perpetual organization – An organization that is without any permanent structure; it takes on whatever form is suitable for current conditions and market demands.

Personalization – Retrieving and structuring knowledge to best meet the preferences and skill set of the knowledge seeker. Popularized as a specific functionality provided in a portal.

Process asset – A set of rules and instructions about a particular process set forth in a methodical and reusable manner. A component of internal awareness.

Process knowledge – The collection of tacit and explicit knowledge relating to the effective execution of a process. The creation of a process asset that ultimately contributes to core competency must include the instinctive, tacit knowledge that contributes to the success of that process. This tacit knowledge can be reduced to a set of rules or converted to explicit knowledge and added to the knowledge base. This process knowledge can then be managed more effectively and contribute to a living knowledge chain of competitive assets that are easily modified as customers and markets change.

Profiling – The creation of online dossiers that track user interest levels and areas of expertise. In an automated approach, profiles are created by monitoring each user's work submitted, work reviewed, and query habits. Profiling is used to feed agent technology, user sensitivity systems, and intermediation systems.

Profit zone – The period of time during which a product's profitability is realized. Knowledge management should provide the practices and culture by which an organization can consistently maintain overlapping product cycles, thereby never falling out of the profit zone. See Organized abandonment.

Return on time (ROT) – A metric for assessing quickly if a knowledge chain is working. Specifically, where P = percentage of profit, sY = sustained years, and nY = number of years:

$$[(P/100) \times (sY/nY)]$$

Single point of access (SPOA) – a desktop front end that provides access to an integrated body of knowledge bases and related processes in a user-customizable fashion. See also Portal.

Single point of search (SPOS) – Also known as federated search, a query tool that accepts a single query and farms it out to one or more knowledge bases, returning a single result set. Typically provided in a portal environment.

Semantic analysis (semiotics) – The analysis of meaning in text. In the context of knowledge management software, a set of analysis programs that identify concepts in documents and their relative importance to the subject of the document and to each other. These utilities form the basis for accurate search and knowledge discovery. See Concept-based search.

Social Network Analysis (SNA) – A form of intermediation. A tool (typically automated) that tracks individual's interaction to create a social map. A social network is a map of the relationships between individuals, indicating the ways in which they are connected through various social familiarities ranging from casual acquaintance to close familial bonds to work projects and areas of interest. SNA can be part of a profiling system.

Socialization – Bringing together of individuals with similar interests. The purpose of communities of practice and communities of interest is to create a vehicle to promote the discovery and sustenance of tacit knowledge by encouraging socialization among individuals with similar knowledge and interests.

Solution brokers – A new class of solution provider. Solution brokers offer a fully integrated solution for most business applications, integrating the component technology with the existing hardware infrastructure, significantly minimizing the risk factors associated with the technology integration.

Structural capital – One of three forms of intellectual capital as defined by Edvinsson and Stewart. Structural capital refers to the value, usually not reflected in accounting systems other than as goodwill, which results from products, systems, or services an organization has built. These may survive the absence of human capital for a period of time (i.e. the brand equity of a popular product), but will soon result in core rigidity without the infusion of human capital. (See Customer capital and Human capital.) A component of internal awareness, structural capital represents the reduction of intellectual capital and customer capital to product or service. The faster you can do this, the greater your structural value, since it does not go stale and become susceptible to competitors.

Suggestive software – Software that is able to deduce a user's knowledge needs and suggest knowledge associations that the user is not able to make.

Tacit knowledge – One of two types of knowledge, whose taxonomy was most notably espoused by Michael Polanyi. Tacit knowledge is experiential know-how based on clues, hunches, instinct, and personal insights, as distinct from formal, explicit knowledge.

Taxonomy – A word-based hierarchical representation of the concepts contained in a body of knowledge. Typically used in portal environments to categorize knowledge objects. See Categorization and Externalization.

Thesaurus – A tool that can be used to increase the efficiency and effectiveness of internalization and externalization tools. The thesaurus is an explicit knowledge resource that documents the lexicon of a body of knowledge or community. A network of words and word meanings and relationships to put conceptual definitions into context. It defines a lexicon and the relationships between words in that lexicon. It can be a precursor to a taxonomy. Thesaurus construction is defined by ANSI standard Z39.19.

Touch points – The priority areas for the application of knowledge management, typically: interactions with customers, interactions with suppliers, and interactions with employees. Each touch point represents an area of potential process or quality improvement and competitive advantage. Touch points represent areas where human interaction is often most intense.

User sensitivity – The ability of an online system to track and manage the experiences and preferences of a user, and to use this knowledge to tailor the delivery of knowledge to that user. Through user sensitivity approaches, the level of communication within a knowledge management system is heightened. See Learning loop.

Velocity of innovation – The rate at which an organization is able to conceive of and introduce new products to market. Innovation is driven by business markets that are battling time to beat their competitors to the next product innovation. The automation of the innovation cycle and resulting decline in time to market is the twenty-first-century equivalent of the automation of production cycles in manufacturing during the better part of the twentieth century. See Return on time and Concept-to-cash.

Virtual organization – A company "without walls" and without many permanent employees; it relies on contractual relationships with suppliers, distributors, and a contingent workforce.

Virtual team – A recombinant structure for work that pulls people and resources together quickly to solve a particular internal or external problem.

Visualization – The ability to visualize a process in intimate detail, capturing parameters about the process that can be used for interpretation, analysis, and discussion. Visualization ideally depicts the process and helps to analyze it. It creates a corporate memory of the process, provides data for analyzing the process, and creates a dynamic framework for a collaborative reengineering of the process.

Work cell – A collection of roles within an organization that crosses functional barriers; individuals in these cells are distinguished by their flexibility and adaptability.

Workflow – One of the tools used for the creation of process assets – a proactive toolset for the analysis, compression, and automation of business activities.

KEY THINKERS IN THE WORLD OF KNOWLEDGE MANAGEMENT

"I use not only the brains I have, but all that I can borrow."

Woodrow Wilson

Davenport, Thomas

Davenport has authored over 15 books pertaining to knowledge management, including the following.

» *Thinking for a Living: How to Get Better Performance and Results from Knowledge workers.* (2005, Harvard Business School Press, Boston)

» *Information Ecology: Mastering the Information and Knowledge Environment* (1997, Oxford University Press, Oxford).

» *Human Capital: What it is and Why People Invest in it* (1999, Jossey-Bass, San Francisco).

» *The Attention Economy: Understanding the New Currency of Business* (1992, Harvard Business School Press, Boston).

» *Working Knowledge: How Organizations Manage What They Know* (2000, Harvard Business School Press, Boston).

Thomas Davenport has also published articles on the subject in *Harvard Business Review*, *Sloan Management Review*, and writes a monthly column for *CIO* magazine. Davenport is currently a Fellow with the Accenture Institute for High Performance Business and holds the President's Chair in Information Technology and Management at Babson College.

Drucker, Peter

The grandfather of all modern thought regarding business, he has been published multiple times over, starting in 1939. To list all of his books and other publications here would cause the length of this title to double. Drucker was the first to emphasize structure and management focused on results, a focus on customers, management by objectives, and decentralized decision making and integrity. Indeed, it was Drucker who first recognized and coined the term "knowledge worker."

Edvinsson, Leif

Co-author of *Intellectual Capital: Realizing Your Company's True Value by Finding Its Hidden Brainpower* (1997, HarperBusiness, New York). Reportedly the first-known CKO. He has been a key contributor to the theory of intellectual capital. As a vice-president and director of intellectual capital at Skandia AFS, he oversaw the creation of the world's first corporate Intellectual Capital Annual Report. In 1996, he won awards from both the American Productivity and Quality Center, USA, and Business Intelligence, UK, for his work on intellectual capital. In 1988, he won the prestigious Brain of the Year award, and now serves as Professor of Intellectual Capital, at Lund University, Sweden.

Nonaka, Ikujiro

Specialist and thought leader in knowledge creation. His research focuses on the creation of the knowledge process in organizations. *The Knowledge Creating Company* (1997, Oxford Press, New York), co-authored with Hirotaka Takeuchi, introduced the world to "organizational knowledge creation," defined as the capability of a company as a whole to create new knowledge, disseminate it throughout the organization, and embody it in products, services, and systems.

According to the authors, it is through this process that organizations can continuously, incrementally, and spirally innovate and grow. Nonaka published several books and papers including the following.

» Knowledge Management, John Wiley & Sons, 2004.
» Handbook of Organizational Learning and Knowledge, Oxford University Press, 2003.
» "Toward middle up-down management: accelerating information creation," *Sloan Management Review*, 1998.
» "The new product development game," *Harvard Business Review*, Jan – Feb, 1986.
» "Creating organizational order out of chaos: self-renewal in Japanese firms," *California Management Review*, Spring, 1998.

Gordon Petrash

Leading visionary and thought leader on Intellectual Asset Property Management (IPAM). Petrash now heads up Petrash Williamson, a consultancy focused on IPAM. **Petrash** was Dow Chemical's first global director of intellectual asset and capital management, where he built and led an organization that increased Dow's intellectual property licensing revenue by 500%, while reducing intellectual property maintenance costs by $50 million.

Polanyi, Michael

A modern day Renaissance man, Polanyi was everything from scientist to philosopher. As a Hungarian medical scientist his research was mainly done in physical chemistry. He turned to philosophy at the age of 55. His works, including *Personal Knowledge* (1974, University of Chicago Press, Chicago), was among the first treatises on how knowledge is created and used. First to identify the difference between tacit and explicit knowledge.

Prusak, Larry

Currently a managing principal with IBM Consulting Services, where he leads the group's research and consults on organizational knowledge issues. He has published widely and has co-authored two books with Thomas Davenport, *Information Ecology* and *Working Knowledge*, and has edited the anthology *Knowledge in Organizations* (1997, Butterworth-Heinemann, Boston). Prior to joining IBM, he was a principal in Ernst & Young's Center for Business Innovation, specializing in issues of corporate knowledge management.

Romer, Paul

Nobel Prize candidate for economics and creator of new growth theory, which positions innovation and creativity at the fulcrum of economic growth. It proposes that in an advanced economy, the most important policies may be the ones that influence the rate of technological innovation in the private sector. Professor Romer's theories have been widely covered in the business press. In 1998 he was named one of America's 25 most influential people by *Time Magazine*, and in 2000 was elected a fellow of American Academy of Arts and Sciences. He is a Professor at Graduate School of Business, Stanford University.

Stewart, Thomas

Stewart pioneered the field of intellectual capital in a series of landmark *Fortune* articles that have earned him an international reputation as a leading expert on the subject. In 1994, the Planning Forum called him "the leading proponent of knowledge management in the business press" and in 1996 he received the International Knowledge Management Awareness Award, presented at the International Knowledge Management Conference in London. His book *Intellectual Capital: The New Wealth of Organizations* was published in 1998 (Diane Publishing Co., Collingdale). In addition to his writing about intellectual capital, he has explored emerging electronic marketplaces, the influence of networks on business, and the economic and management implications of the Information Age.

Hubert Saint-Onge

The founder and Principal of **SaintOnge** Alliance. In addition to holding key senior management positions in leading companies over the past 25 years, he has developed and refined a model called the Knowledge Assets Framework. This model strategically integrates business plans with branding, leadership and people management in order to optimize the performance of an organization.

Sveiby, Karl Erik

A principal of a global network of consultants, known as Sveiby Knowledge Associates (SKA) and professor in Knowledge Management at the Swedish Business School in Helsinki. Sveiby is one of Scandinavia's best-known management consultants. His published works include the following.

» *Managing Knowhow* (1987, Bloomsbury, London).
» *The Invisible Balance Sheet* (1988, Ledarskap, Stockholm).
» *Manager in Creative Environments* (1991, Dagblade, Stockholm).
» *The Knowledge Organization* (1994, Celemi, Stockholm).
» *The New Organizational Wealth: Managing and Measuring Knowledge-based Assets* (1997, Berrett-Koehler, San Francisco).

09

Resources for Knowledge Management

Embark into the world of knowledge management and you will quickly discover that you are not alone. Traditional and cyber-based resources abound, including:

» books;
» periodicals;
» portals;
» Websites;
» institutes of higher learning; and
» associations.

"The pace and nature of change means that everyone must engage in lifelong learning"

Gerald Hoffman, author of Technology Payoff

For those that want to get more engulfed in the issues of knowledge management, there are ample resources of various kinds to lull you in.

Note: Books authored and listed by the knowledge thinkers profiled in Chapter 8 have not been listed here but are, of course, excellent resources.

BOOKS

Allee, V. (1997) *The Knowledge Evolution, Building Organizational Intelligence*. Butterworth-Heinemann, Boston. Provides an introduction to understanding knowledge creation, learning, and performance in everyday work. It includes best practices from leading-edge companies, essential guidelines, design principles, analogies, and conceptual frameworks.

Amidon, D. (1997) *Innovation Strategy for the Knowledge Economy, The Ken Awakening*. Butterworth-Heinemann, Boston. This is one of five books from Debra Amidon, thought leader on innovation. It provides practical as well as theoretical views of innovation strategy. It does not deal with barriers, hurdles, or conflicts to be resolved; rather, it provides a vision of how you can take advantage of collective learning to move an enterprise forward.

Applehans, Globe and Laugero (1998) *Managing Knowledge: A Practical Web-based Approach*. Addison-Wesley, Boston. Takes a look at the role of enterprise content in a knowledge base, and offers advise on how to determine what belongs in the knowledge base.

Buckman, Robert (2004) Building a Knowledge Driven Organization, McGraw-Hill Companies, New York. This book is written by the former leader of Buckman Laboratories, a pioneer in knowledge-driven organizations. The book focuses on what it takes to get knowledge workers to contribute to a knowledge system. This is a primer on how managers and employees can change habits and mentality to move from a knowledge hoarding environment and culture to one of openness and sharing.

Cortada and Woods (eds) (2000) *The Knowledge Management Yearbook 1999–2000*. Butterworth-Heinemann, Boston. This work is a collection of over 40 articles written by many leading experts on knowledge management. Topics include strategy, organizational learning, tools and techniques.

Cunningham, M.J. (2001) *Partners.com: How to profit from the DNA of Business*. Perseus Publishing, Cambridge. Cunningham explains how a business can forge Web-based partnerships (knowledge-based collaboration) with competitors, customers, employees, suppliers, and distributors to create an extended value chain. Topics such as vortals and exchanges are discussed.

Dixon, N. (2000) *Common Knowledge: How Companies Thrive by Sharing What They Know*. Harvard Business School Press, Boston. Focuses on the internal awareness practices of an organization, or what the author calls common knowledge. It provides insights as to the value of this knowledge and methods for assembling and managing this knowledge base.

Harvard Business Review (1998) *The Harvard Business Review on Knowledge Management*. Harvard Business School Press, Boston. This is a compilation of many of the papers written by many of the leading thinkers in knowledge management and published in the *Harvard Business Review*. Includes Peter Drucker's "The Coming of the New Organization" and Ikujiro Nonaka's "The Knowledge-Creating Company."

Koulopoulos, T., Spinello and Toms (1997) *Corporate Instinct: Building a Knowing Enterprise for the 21st Century*. Van Nostrand Reinhold, New York. This work talked about knowledge management in a practical business setting when many were still treating knowledge management as an academic issue. It introduces the idea of the knowledge chain, a way to measure the rate of innovation in your organization.

Koulopoulos, T. and Palmer, N. (2001) *The X-Economy*. Texere, New York. This work does not focus on knowledge management per se, but the exchange economy, extended value chains, and innovation – all topics that emanate from organizations that are entrenched in knowledge management.

McGovern, M. and Russell, D. (2001) *A New Brand of Expertise*. Butterworth-Heinemann, Boston. This book explores the role of independent experts in the new economy. It is a great treatise on the value of free agency from the perspective of corporate buyer and consultant. Its authors describe how businesses are currently using this resource, and provide strategies for both experienced and new independent consultants.

Myers, P.S. (1996) *Knowledge Management and the Organizational Design*. Butterworth-Heinemann, Boston. Takes a hard-nose look at how knowledge management affects and is effected by organizational structure and bureaucracy. The role and power of innovation, collaboration (both internally and externally), organizational learning and incentivizing knowledge sharing are discussed.

Shuman, J., Twombly, J. and Rottenberg, D. (2001) *Collaborative Communities: Partnering for Profit in the Networked Economy*. Dearborn Trade, Chicago. Looks specifically at the knowledge management practice of collaboration across enterprises as a way to build an extended value chain, and organize a business around clients, suppliers and partners.

Tannenbaum and Alliger (2000) *Knowledge Management: Clarifying the Key Issues*. Created as a compilation of articles written by the authors for the *IHRIM* journal, this book provides a primer on basic knowledge management concepts and ideas.

Zack, M. (1999) *Knowledge and Strategy*. Butterworth-Heinemann, Oxford. Links the topics of knowledge management and business strategy. It centers on the concept of treating organizational knowledge as a valuable strategy asset.

PERIODICALS, WEBSITES AND PORTALS

The Ark Group
(http://www.ark-group.com/home/km/)

The Ark Group is an international organization that produces publications and events in three basic areas, one being knowledge management. This group publishes 2 periodicals: *ei magazine* (an archive of case studies, detailing the successes and failures of information-management strategies); and *Inside Knowledge* (an array of articles covering a broad range of knowledge management issues.)

Association of Knowledge (AOK) (www.kwork.org)

This cyber association was started (and is still managed) by Jerry Ash in January 2000. It is focused on knowledge management and its application in the business setting. It offers free access and access to additional resources for paying association members. Features a bookstore, a "library," white papers and articles, discussion groups, and networking. And an expert panel called K911. Their purpose, as stated on their Website is "to provide a venue around which knowledge and ideas about knowledge work can flow across disciplines and hierarchies; to synthesize individual and collective thinking into new collaborative knowledge; to transform a growing body of knowledge into practical models of knowledge work strategies and practice; to promote the interdisciplinary art of KW through the intellect of a unified voice; and to provide products and services that will assist members in managing the knowledge asset."

@Brint.com

This is an excellent resource for the person interested in exploring knowledge management from many perspectives. It is a knowledge management portal offering a plethora of articles, threaded discussions and thought pieces available for download. Its mission, as stated on the site, is "developing leading-edge thinking and practice on contemporary business, technology and knowledge management issues to facilitate organizational and individual performance, success and fulfillment."

BulletPoint Online (www.bulletpoint.com)

This is an online periodical focused on business management issues such as teamwork, leadership, change, and innovation. Topics are researched/surveyed and information is distilled and condensed into a short, skimmable format geared to senior business management.

CIO Magazine – the Knowledge Management Research Center (www.cio.com/research/knowledge)

The KM Research Center of the *CIO* online magazine focuses on a few links to content from *CIO* and Websites that focus on late-breaking knowledge management topics. It provides access to articles, Websites, forums, glossary and white papers. The content/offers are arranged into strategy, measurement, process, technology, books, events, metrics, and vendors' categories.

Delphi Group (www.delphigroup.com)

Strategic business advisors and technology market makers focusing on the intersection of business and technology – what they call biztech. Delphi Group's core competencies are in the emerging technologies of knowledge management, collaborative commerce, portals, content management, enterprise wireless, and e-learning. They deliver that insight and expertise through four distinct channels: market research and publications; educational seminars, industry events and customized onsite seminars; strategic consulting including the execution of knowledge audits; and market advisory services to vendors of technology.

Destination KM (www.destinationKM.com)

This is an archival site for past issues of Knowledge Management Magazine and destination KM. Now managed by Line 56 media, the site provides access to past content focused on Knowledge Management in a business setting.

EContent magazine (www.ecmag.net)

This magazine is available online and in paper. It is a great resource focused on content management, with a knowledge management component growing in importance. EContent magazine is the premier source for strategies and resources for the digital content industry. It is positioned to mid- to senior-level executives involved in strategic issues related to content creation, acquisition, organization, and distribution in B2B or B2C environments or within their own organizations.

The Eknowledge center (www.eknowledgecenter.com)

An online knowledge management university. The center provides KM training and coaching.

Global Knowledge Innovation Infrastructure
(www.entovation.com/gkii)

This is an international knowledge management forum that provides online sources and meets as an organization. Membership is required. From their Website: "The GKII is an exciting initiative to build the foundations for creating innovation capabilities that will deliver prosperity in the 21st century knowledge economy." It draws together people and organizations from different industries, different functions and different geographies in a collaborative programme of learning, research and practical action."

Insitiute for Intellectual Capital Research IICR
(http://www.intellectualcapital.nl/)

This web site provides access to a list of the prominent researchers in the intellectual capital management. It also identifies organizations and knowledge managers in the process of developing intellectual capital strategies and systems. It also is a gateway to published best practices, conferences, lessons learned, intellectual capital metrics, assessment tools and knowledge management software packages.

Intelligent Enterprise Magazine
(www.intelligententerprise.com)

Intelligent Enterprise is a magazine focused on the application of technologies in realistic business applications to provide strategic applications. Issues are covered from both the context and the technical perspective.

Journal of Intellectual Capital
(www.emeraldinsight.com/info/journals/
jic/jic.htm)

This journal is academically focused, but valuable to business as well. In their words, "The *Journal of Intellectual Capital* is dedicated to the international exchange of cutting-edge research and best practice on all aspects of managing intellectual capital in organizations." While focusing on the identification and implementation of innovative intellectual capital strategies, this journal also addresses the application of theoretical concepts to the modern knowledge economy.

KMCi (Knowledge Management Consortium International (www.kmci.org)

A non-profit association of KM professionals from around the world. Includes training and online bookstore.

KM Institute (www.kminstitute.org)

This is the web site for the KM Institute, a KM Training and Solutions Provider. On the web site you can access many papers focused on applying KM into a professional setting. The institute provides KM Certification Programs for all levels of KM competence.

KMPro (http://kmpro.org/)

KMPro is a non-profit organization serving the professional needs of the international Knowledge Management community. This is a member-centric organization, working locally and globally, to invigorate the KM community by promoting KM awareness, support & development of KM best practices, and advancement of KM research and development.

Knowledge Management News (http://www.kmnews.com/)

This is a free ezine and occasional newsletter focused on Knowledge, Contnet, Information and Identity Management.

Knowledge Management Resource Center (www.kmresource.com)

This is a knowledge management portal. This site offers a collection of knowledge management resources, each of them reviewed and briefly described to expedite the selection process. Resources (white papers, book references, and articles) are categorized into 17 areas including: introduction to knowledge management, case studies, products and services, search engines and portals, and periodicals.

Knowledge Nurture (www.knowledge-nurture.com)

This Website was developed by Buckman Laboratories, a specialty chemicals company whose former CEO, Robert Buckman, is a knowledge management champion. This site is based on knowledge management work done at Buckman Labs, and provides resources for individuals who want to start their knowledge management education.

Knowledge Shop (www.knowledgeshop.com)

This is a one stop store for everything knowledge management. Products for purchase include ISO standards, books and whitepapers, novelty items (pens and coffee mugs), methodologies and toolkits, learning aids and conferences/seminars.KnowMap (www.knowmap.com)

KnowMap: The Knowledge Management, Auditing and Mapping Magazine is a bimonthly web-based journal targeted at knowledge management practitioners, covering tangible tools and methods for strategy development and implementation of knowledge management initiatives.

Mywiseowl.com (www.mywiseowl.com/articles/ Knowledge_management)

This is a knowledge management portal that provides an overview of the subject and links to many related topics and issues.

UNIC Universal Networking intellectual capital (www.unic.net)

This is a portal focused on intellectual capital and its management. It was inspired and is funded by Leif Edvisson. The portal serves as a collaborative exchange of ideas on intellectual capital.

Ten Steps to Making Knowledge Management Work

Though no two knowledge management practices will be exactly the same, there are critical, common steps to implementation that should be practiced. Guidance is given on the following ten steps that help to guarantee the success of a knowledge management initiative:

» defining the community;
» strategy and critical success factor development;
» the knowledge audit;
» ROI;
» knowledge leadership;
» execution of core competencies;
» knowledge inventories;
» promoting informal practices;
» building an ecosystem ripe with incentivization plans; and
» supplying an infrastructure and building a cyclical practice.

"The great end of life is not knowledge, but action."
Thomas Henry Huxley

Though no two knowledge practices will be exactly the same, and no two will evolve in precisely the same way, there are basic steps that should be taken in order to increase your success with knowledge management. Below, I have outlined 10 such steps.

1. DEFINE THE COMMUNITY

As simple and obvious as this may seem, start your knowledge management initiative by reflecting for whom this initiative is being undertaken. Knowledge management solutions should be carefully designed and developed for a particular audience. There is no one-size-fits-all solution. Indeed, if the audience is diverse enough, you may create a single solution, but one that has many components and customized front ends, each created to specifically satisfy the needs of groups and individuals.

2. DEFINE A STRATEGY AND CRITICAL SUCCESS FACTORS

Once you have determined for whom the knowledge management practice will be developed, establish a clear and well-communicated strategy or purpose for the program. As Michael Porter puts it, "Having a strategy is a matter of discipline. It requires a strong focus on profitability rather than just growth, an ability to define a unique value proposition and a willingness to make tough trade-offs in choosing what not to do." As Porter stresses, your strategy is equally about what not to do as well as what to do. As discussed in Chapter 6, the strategy must include a series of critical success factors (CSFs). The CSFs will not only guide your implementation and measurement processes – they will also serve as benchmarks against which a business case and cost justification can be executed. (See Chapter 6 for a discussion and definition of CSFs.)

3. EXECUTE A KNOWLEDGE AUDIT

The audience and the plan are now carefully defined. But bigger, equally critical questions remain. For the same reasons that you must define who the audience is, you must assess the current state of that audience, its business practices, its propensity for knowledge management, value seen in knowledge, current knowledge production and usage habits. These issues and others need to be identified and measured using a knowledge audit. Call it an audit, call it a map, call it a diagnosis. The purpose of the audit is to understand the constraints, discover the tacit and explicit sources of knowledge, and surface the opportunities for, and obstacles to, knowledge work.

Remember, first and foremost, knowledge management is about how people share and use what they know. You must become intimate with individual and collective needs and attitudes regarding knowledge sharing and innovation. Audits must involve virtually everyone in the population identified in step 1. The audit should determine what, if any, knowledge sharing already exists in an organization and what type of knowledge is considered valuable by staff. Communication protocols, attitudes regarding sharing and approaches to collaboration should be uncovered through an audit. Users' aptitudes to embrace knowledge and use it strategically must be assessed. Factors that motivate individuals to not only contribute/share knowledge but also seek it out and redeploy it in creative new ways must also be understood. Knowledge management exists in every organization. It does not need a formal practice. Formal knowledge management initiatives/practices augment and leverage what already exists in the organization, and thus maximize the potential.

Several factors should be measured separately, and in conjunction with the others, offering a unique profile of every organization's effectiveness and opportunity in applying KM (see Fig. 10.1). This profile offers insights as to how your organization ranks relative to others in your industry, or even how different groups within one organization rank against each other's use of KM. The resulting benchmarks can be used to justify, measure ROI, and precisely assess the value of KM.

In Fig. 10.1, the organization profiled with the dotted line has little in the way of formal KM technology or practices, yet it demonstrates an ideal environment for leveraging KM practices and technologies. The organization profiled with the dark black line has KM technology and practices, yet demonstrates an organizational environment that

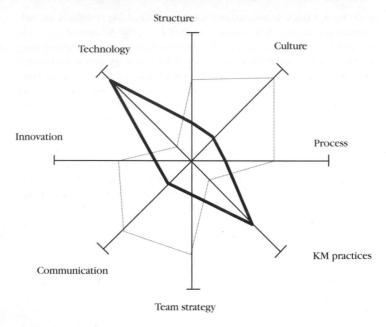

Fig. 10.1 Knowledge audit profiles of two organizations' effectiveness and opportunity in applying KM.

undermines its KM efforts. Neither organization is ideal. Understanding where and how to overcome the inadequacies of each organization is the purpose of a knowledge audit.

Lastly, the methodology used should uncover organizational anomalies among the organization-wide findings, and uncover groups within the organization that exhibit positive and negative variances in each of the factors measured. In this manner, you uncover potential points of strength, weakness or opportunity for knowledge management within your organization.

In this manner, a strategy that includes an intelligent approach to understanding the changes required in culture as well as technology can be derived. I have witnessed firsthand the incredible results of knowledge audits in our own practice. In one case, the results of an audit affected the turnaround at an R&D department at a major petrochemical company. They had embarked on several knowledge-based initiatives, each of which had full support from upper management. Despite this, the organization's ability to reuse acquired know-how and expertise had not been impacted. The application of the knowledge audit uncovered several obstacles that the efforts to date had ignored. These included cultural differences across various geographic locations, discrepancies in "management speak" versus "management action," and process realities that flew in the face of knowledge-sharing practices. The audit also uncovered an underlying cultural approach to team building, which had been virtually untapped by initiatives. Once these strengths and weaknesses were identified, an action plan was developed specifically to handle and exploit them respectively. As a result, minor modifications to existing systems brought about major changes and a real ROI.

In yet another instance, the audit revealed that, despite high achievement in internal and external awareness levels (see Chapter 2 for more detail on internal and external awareness), in this manufacturing company, bodies of knowledge were treated as isolated silos. Thus, despite the levels of knowledge acquired, the overall organization reacted lethargically to changes in stimuli, and required extensive corporate review and approval. Exceptions existed in the form of informal teams that arose almost organically within the organization. By uncovering the obstacles as well as the strengths, minor modifications in technology directions and communication protocols were set in place that enabled this organization to achieve radically positive results.

In the final analysis, the knowledge audit may be the smartest thing you do to leverage your organization's knowledge. The audit process is applicable to small companies as well as large corporations. Too often smaller organizations falsely believe they can escape a knowledge audit because the close proximity of workers automatically facilitates knowledge sharing. For example, I know of one firm of 50 that felt this way. But upon close scrutiny, we determined that, despite a facade of constant sharing, there was often reluctance to completely share and collaborate. Employees felt their individual worth was more determined by what they knew and others did not, rather than what was known as a whole. This perception was reinforced, unintentionally but consistently, by management in the job descriptions, annual reviews, pay scales and the language used in memos. Yes, larger organizations may face physical distribution challenges, but these pale when compared to communication protocol, incentive, process and leadership style issues. Compare the following real-world companies.

Company A, a worldwide metals extrusion and refining company, suffered from language and time differences, but its employees often spoke of co-workers as family. There was a general tendency, supported by management, to seek out the advice and know-how of others in the organization. Technology was put in place to expedite the ability to make a request for collaboration. Culture supported these requests with rapid and frequent responses. As a result, formal and informal networks of like-minded individuals from around the globe formed and were reinforced daily.

Company B, a professional services company located within a single building in the USA, was comprised of over 100 employees. Although staff spoke of co-workers, they did so in the way that co-workers actually *belonged* to specific departments (implying who harbored different agendas). Despite the constant direct interaction with fellow employees on a regular basis, Company B had a far greater knowledge management set of issues before it than Company A.

Smaller organizations may have fewer participants to lead and mentor into a knowledge-based practice, but they face all the same potential issues as a larger organization.

4. IF NECESSARY, EXECUTE AN ROI

With the results of the audit behind you, you can now move forward with deliberate steps to build and maintain the knowledge management practice in your organization. Step 4 is an optional step – but in some companies it may be necessary. I am speaking of performing a formal return on investment (ROI). Steps 1–3 provide you with the raw material needed to perform such an analysis. If you need to execute this step, refer to Chapter 8 for more detail on ROI.

5. DETERMINE THE RIGHT APPROACH TO KNOWLEDGE LEADERSHIP FOR YOUR ORGANIZATION

Next, your attention should shift to management issues. Based on what you have learned in the audit, make a decision as to the type of leadership you will need to champion the knowledge cause and manage it going forward. (For more details regarding the role of a CKO, and alternatives, refer to Chapter 8.)

But, go beyond definition of the knowledge management practice leader itself. Look to the audit to help define best and worst practices in line management for cultivating and promoting knowledge sharing and innovation. Though not managers of the knowledge practice per se, our research and experience have found that, 90 percent of the time, front-line managers and their style of leadership have an immediate impact on the knowledge culture of a team. There is no best way for such a manager to operate, universally. But within your organization you will find those approaches that work and those that do not. Formalize/train on those that work and abate those that do not.

6. IDENTIFY AND AGREE UPON THE CORE COMPETENCIES OF THE ORGANIZATION

As discussed in Chapter 2, it is around your core competencies that you should fashion your knowledge practice, not core products. Simple to do? No. And too often organizations forget this step. Consider what happened to many of the brick and mortar companies that made folly into the world of dot-com. Many forgot what their unique value statement was and rushed to implement Web-based versions of their business, copying the dot-com start-up competitors. They lost their distinction and did not leverage their years of know-how – and customer relations. For example, consider Merrill Lynch, which undermined its most precious resource – the knowledge embodied in its brokers – with the advent of its dot-com site. This knowledge was the product and should have been leveraged, not facilitated access to the stock market.

7. TAKE AN INVENTORY OF THE KNOWLEDGE SOURCES THE COMMUNITY USES, AND THOSE IT DOES NOT USE

Determine why it does not use these knowledge sources and challenge that decision. Identify each knowledge source as explicit or tacit. For those that are tacit, determine if they can be made implicit (see Chapter 2 for definitions of explicit, tacit and implicit knowledge).

Determine the best means to organize the collection of knowledge and make it assessable (see Chapter 6 for details on categorization and technology available to assist in this task). Determine the best approach to tracking sources of tacit knowledge and utilize intermediation software as applicable (see Chapter 4 for more details on intermediation software.)

The bottom line is to be sure that content provided in your knowledge initiative holds significance and value to its audience right from the start, or the initiative will clearly crash and burn.

8. DETERMINE THE QUALITY OF EXISTING INFORMAL KNOWLEDGE PRACTICES

Use the outcome of the audit to determine the presence and quality of informal knowledge practices already at work in the organization. Grapevines, interpersonal networks, after-hours social groups, unofficial meetings – these are all examples of knowledge management at work. Identify the best practices among them and fortify them. Encourage and promote them. Identify any that may run counter to your critical success factors (e.g. a "good ole boy" network that is exclusionary) and make efforts to abate and eventually eliminate them.

9. BUILD AN ECOSYSTEM RIPE WITH INCENTIVIZATION

In building a knowledge-sharing community, there needs to exist personal desire to share knowledge. In one pharmaceutical company I audited, for example, there existed a very strong knowledge-sharing culture. Individuals used words such as "family" and "united cause" when speaking of their relationship with co-workers. Knowledge was freely shared. You may think that this organization had few problems to overcome with regards to incentivization, but this conclusion is short sighted. Despite the willingness to share, there was no incentive to do so. Sharing occurred if and when a co-worker asked for knowledge. But, despite the creation of elaborate knowledge-based systems, virtually no one was taking the time nor making the effort to formally store their knowledge into these systems to promote wide-scale accessibility. The reasons for this were not based in a tendency to hoard, but rather a lack of reason to make this extra effort. Employees did not see knowledge sharing as part of their formal job description, did not see management recognizing it as part of the work effort, did not feel they were recognized for doing it. Therefore, while from a cultural and personal standpoint they were all willing to share what they knew, in a formal capacity it wasn't happening.

Establish a knowledge metric, a standard to how your organization recognizes knowledge sharing. Until your metric is well defined and understood, any attempts at defining a method of incentivization can prove futile. Look at this as a means to recognize people for their efforts in sharing knowledge and in advertising the success of knowledge management to the rest of the organization.

First and foremost, individuals need to know what constitutes a knowledge transfer or sharing. There are at least three popular techniques that you can choose from – only one is likely to help in my experience: input (knowledge sharing could be measured by the frequency of input to the system), output (recognition is given for re-purposing existing knowledge to promote new ideas, processes and/or products), and input/output cycles (what is recognized are the connections that result in action, collaboration between knowledge provider and user). Whatever approach you take, it is important to consider recognizing knowledge sharing in the context of communities. This helps to create bonds of trust, as it challenges the individual belief of knowledge as power by encouraging community sharing.

Once a metric is established and understood, establish a method of Incentivization. In other words, why would the users want to be recognized under the metric plan? The method of incentivization must be customized to meet each organization's needs, both those of management and those of end users. The following is a list of some forms of incentivization that have worked.

» Link it to performance/project reviews – make knowledge sharing and usage a defined part of job descriptions and formal reviews.
» Awards or plaques – often, simple recognition of a job well done is enough to motivate workers. This is especially true in organizations that have a strong culture towards personal esteem but, in any case, it requires sincerity and personalization behind the award. Do not mail the award – it should be presented by senior management personally, and with some fanfare.
» Time – employees who work in a production oriented/nose-to-the-grindstone culture often point to being given official time to impart what they know, and/or search for what others know, as all the incentive they need to use the system.
» Money and prizes/remuneration – while you may eschew direct monetary reward as a means of incentivization, in some instances it can work – it just is not always necessary. This is particularly true in cases where you need to jump-start an initiative.

10. SUPPLY AN INFRASTRUCTURE AND THE MEANS TO IMPROVE

This is a multi-part step and makes this 10-step exercise somewhat cyclical. Put in place technology, as applicable, to support the efforts. Technology should simplify the process of knowledge discovery and knowledge sharing. Community members should not have to "work at" knowledge sharing. It should come as a by-product of work production. This is the ultimate role of technology, to act as facilitator and enabler, not a solution. As part of the facilitation process, look to ways to measure success, and rewards (augment steps 9 and 4 above). Put in place matrices to measure and re-examine the strategy, and then rework the strategy. Knowledge management strategy is an ongoing effort that should be evergreen. This is the primary responsibility of the knowledge leader, as opposed to the tactical work of the front-line managers. As you become indoctrinated with this approach to strategy, remember the words of T.S. Eliot: "We shall not cease from exploration, and the end of all our exploring will be to arrive where we started and know the place for the first time.''

KEY LEARNING POINTS

There are ten steps or practices that help to guarantee the success of a knowledge management initiative.

1 Define the community.
2 Define a strategy and critical success factors.
3 Execute a knowledge audit.
4 If necessary, execute an ROI.
5 Determine the right approach to knowledge leadership for your organization:
   » executive level;
   » front-line managers.
6 Define and bolster core competencies.
7 Conduct a knowledge inventory:
   » explicit sources;
   » tacit sources;
   » implicit sources;
   » categorization.
8 Identify and promote positive informal practices; abate the bad.
9 Build an ecosystem ripe with incentivization plans.
10 Supply an infrastructure and create a series of benchmarks and measurement procedures to keep the practice evergreen.

Frequently Asked Questions (FAQs)

Q1: What is knowledge management?

A: See Chapter 2 for a succinct definition, as well as a broad description.

Q2: How do you initiate a knowledge management practice?

A: See Chapter 10 (point 3) for a discussion of the knowledge audit process.

Q3: How do you determine your specific needs for knowledge management and develop a ROI?

A: See Chapters 6 and 10 (points 1 and 2) for the role of critical success factors, measuring intellectual capital, and the return on innovation.

Q4: How critical is culture to the success of knowledge management?

A: See Chapters 5 and 6 (sub-section on culture) for insight on how to manage regional and corporate culture.

Q5: What are the differences between core competencies and core products, and which should I be more concerned about?

A: See Chapter 2 (sub-section on grapevines, communities of practices and the informal knowledge network, and internal awareness) and Chapter 10 (point 6).

Q6: How do you encourage individuals to share knowledge?

A: See Chapter 10 (point 9) for a discussion on effective incentive plans.

Q7: What is the knowledge chain, and how do I use it to determine my organization's rate of innovation?

A: See Chapter 2 (sub-section on the knowledge chain) for a definition and examples of best and worst practices.

Q8: What is the difference between explicit, tacit and implicit knowledge?

A: See Chapter 2 (sub-section on the complexity of knowledge: from explicit to tacit) for a definition and comparison.

Q9: What type of leadership is required of a knowledge management practice? Does it require a chief knowledge officer (CKO)?

A: See Chapter 6 (sub-section on knowledge and leadership – is a CKO necessary?) for an explanation of the need for leadership, definition of the CKO, and alternatives.

Q10: What role can technology play in a knowledge management practice?

A: See Chapter 4 for a full discussion on this topic.

Acknowledgments

I thank my family, Ann, Anna and Teresa, for sharing their lives with me. I thank the staff of Delphi Group, for their support of my efforts, not only with this title, but in all that I do. Their teamwork and comradeship is one of my most valuable resources. I thank all of my clients, who have allowed me to share knowledge with them and grow along the way. Lastly, thank you to Capstone Publishers, for making the sharing of my knowledge possible in this medium.

Index